MACMILLAN

Middlemarch

Retold by Margaret Tarner

MACMILLAN READERS
UPPER LEVEL

Founding Editor: John Milne

The Macmillan Readers provide a choice of enjoyable reading materials for learners of English. The series is published at six levels – Starter, Beginner, Elementary, Pre-intermediate, Intermediate and Upper.

Level Control
Information, structure and vocabulary are controlled to suit the students' ability at each level.

The number of words at each level:

Starter	about 300 basic words
Beginner	about 600 basic words
Elementary	about 1100 basic words
Pre-intermediate	about 1400 basic words
Intermediate	about 1600 basic words
Upper	about 2200 basic words

Vocabulary
Some difficult words and phrases in this book are important for understanding the story. Some of these words are explained in the story, some are shown in the pictures, and others are marked with a number like this: ...[3]. Words with a number are explained in the Glossary at the end of the book.

Answer Keys
An Answer Key for the *Points for Understanding* section and help with answers to the *Further Study Questions* can be found at www.macmillanenglish.com/readers

Contents

	A Note About The Author	4
	A Note About This Story	5
1	Two Sisters	8
2	Two Letters	12
3	Middlemarch	16
4	Doctor Lydgate	21
5	A Meeting in Rome	25
6	Home Again	29
7	An Engagement	35
8	A Funeral and a Will	39
9	The Cousins	44
10	Plans	51
11	The Answer	56
12	Power Beyond the Grave	63
13	Marriage Problems	73
14	The Last Goodbye?	78
15	Money Matters	85
16	Temptation	92
17	The Secret is Out	96
18	Two Wives	103
19	Dorothea Makes Some Decisions	107
20	True Conversations	113
21	After the Storm	116
22	What Came Afterwards	121
	Points for Understanding	125
	Glossary	131
	Further Study Questions	138

A Note About The Author

George Eliot was born in 1819. Her real name was Mary Ann (later Marian) Evans. The third of three children, she was born on a farm in the English Midlands where her father looked after an estate[1] owned by a rich landowner.

Mary Ann was plain, but she was very intelligent. She went to a good boarding school[2] where her talent for writing poetry and fiction was admired. When Mary Ann was 19, her mother died and she had to return home to look after her father. She was afraid that she would never have a chance for a life of her own. However, her father encouraged her to continue her education at home, and in 1841 he and his daughter moved to Coventry. There Mary Ann met the intellectual[3] couple, Charles and Cara Bray. Through this friendship, Mary Ann also met other well-known thinkers and writers of the time.

In 1849, Mary Ann's father died, and she moved to London. There she met the publisher and bookseller, John Chapman, who asked her to edit a journal called *The Westminster Review*. She did this work for the following two years and the journal became very successful.

In 1851, Mary Ann met the writer George Henry Lewes, who encouraged her to write fiction. Lewes and Mary Ann quickly fell in love. Lewes was married, but he could not get a divorce so, in 1854, he and Mary Ann decided to live together. This was a very shocking thing to do at that time and many people refused to meet them. But some of the most well known writers of the time remained their friends and the couple stayed together until Lewes died.

Mary Ann began writing stories when she was thirty-eight. She called herself George Eliot. She chose a man's name, because she wanted to be taken seriously as a writer. At that time, most women wrote romantic stories and Mary Ann wanted to write about 'real' people. In 1858, Mary Ann published her first novel

Adam Bede, and it was an immediate success. She went on writing for another fifteen years, publishing the great classics *The Mill on the Floss* (1860), *Silas Marner* (1861), *Middlemarch* (1871–2) and *Daniel Deronda* (1876). She always wrote under the name George Eliot, even though most people knew who she really was.

George Lewes died in 1878 and two years later, Mary Ann married a much younger man. But after only a few months of a happy married life, George Eliot herself died and was buried next to George Lewes.

A Note About This Story

Middlemarch was written in 1871–2 and first published in eight monthly parts. It was a great success and was published as a complete book in 1874. It was George Eliot's most important work.

Middlemarch was based on the small Midlands town of Coventry (now a major city) where Eliot lived as a young woman. At that time, Coventry was a place of many social classes, where people were often closely related to each other and were suspicious of strangers. And like all people in small towns, the people of Middlemarch loved to gossip[4]. Most new ideas were criticised[5] and change was not welcomed.

But at the time when the novel took place – between 1829 and 1833 – many changes were coming to towns like Coventry and no one could stop them. The Reform Bill[6] of 1832 changed Parliament[7] and allowed more people to vote. Travel was made easier by the railways and the countryside was changed by the building of new industrial cities.

Middlemarch started as two different stories, one about Dorothea Brooke and the other about the young Doctor Lydgate. Then Eliot decided to put the two stories together, giving both characters equal importance. There are many themes in *Middlemarch*, but the most important one is that of marriage and what men and women of that time expected from it.

The heroine, Dorothea, is very rich and very beautiful. She lives with her rich uncle, Mr Brooke, and her younger sister, Celia, in a big old house in the countryside near Middlemarch. Mr Brooke is a rich landowner who loves talking about doing good, but actually does very little for his tenants or his land. His older niece, Dorothea, is intelligent, but uneducated. At that time, the usual intention of rich young women was to marry a rich man with land and a big house. Therefore, Dorothea and her sister have very little to do. Servants look after everything for them.

But Dorothea wants to use her intelligence and she wants her life to have a real purpose. So she marries an older man, Edward Casaubon, because she admires his mind and believes that she can help him with the book he has spent his life writing. But Dorothea soon finds married life a disappointment, because her husband cannot love her and he believes that all women have inferior[8] minds. When Casaubon dies, Dorothea finds real love with Will Ladislaw, a young man related to her first husband, but different from him in every way. Will is a rebel[9] and a stranger to the town of Middlemarch.

Young Doctor Lydgate, another newcomer to the town, makes a bad marriage although he does much good in Middlemarch. He falls in love with the silly, selfish beauty Rosamond Vincy, who prevents him from achieving his ambitions[10].

The plain, straightforward Mary Garth, a farmer's daughter, marries for love. However, she only agrees to marry Fred Vincy, Rosamond's brother, when he decides to work hard and forget about having money.

Eliot linked these stories together and showed her readers that marriage does not always lead to happiness or true understanding. She also showed how unkind and mean people can be to others who are different from themselves.

Although Eliot wrote about a different time and a different society in *Middlemarch*, the book is still popular today because people do not really change. The same themes and issues that were important then are still important now. We all have the same hopes and fears. We all have to learn from our mistakes and be able to help each other – in order to make our own lives truly happy.

1
Two Sisters

'Dorothea, dear, why don't you stop working for a minute?' Celia asked her elder sister when they were sitting together one afternoon. 'You know that your eyes are not strong and you have been drawing those plans for over an hour.'

'But they are for Sir James. I must finish them,' Dorothea replied. 'I am so glad that he asked me to make the plans for the new cottages[11] in Freshitt village. I want to show him how well I can do it.'

Celia sighed. Then she said, 'There is something that I'd like to do, if you're not too busy.'

'What is it, dear?' Dorothea asked. 'Is anything wrong?'

'No, of course not. But I thought we could look at mamma's jewels[12],' Celia replied, 'You have the key to her jewellery box in your desk. Don't you remember? Our uncle gave us the jewels exactly six months ago and we still haven't looked at them.'

Dorothea looked at her sister in surprise. 'Why do you want to see them?' she asked. 'We don't need to see mamma's jewels to be reminded of her, Celia.'

Celia blushed[13] and she turned her pretty face away. 'I was wondering if we could wear them sometimes,' she said quietly, 'to show that we haven't forgotten mamma. And... our uncle is having guests for dinner tonight, as you know. One of them is Sir James Chettam. We should try to look our best.'

Dorothea opened her beautiful eyes very wide. 'I see. I didn't know that you wanted to wear the jewels,' she said with a smile.

She put down her pencil and stood up, then walked across the room to her desk and took out the key. She picked up the beautiful wooden jewellery box and carried it carefully across the room.

Two Sisters

'There you are, Celia,' Dorothea said, putting the big box on the table and unlocking it.

Soon the table was covered with sparkling jewels. Dorothea picked up a beautiful gold necklace set with purple amethysts.

'This will suit you, dear,' she said to her sister. 'Let me put it on for you.'

Celia looked at herself in the mirror. The purple jewels shone with a clear light against the gold.

'Yes, I shall wear this necklace tonight,' Celia said. 'But what about you, Dorothea? You must wear something pretty too. Look, these pearls do not shine so much, but they are very lovely.'

Dorothea shook her head and opened a smaller box. Inside, was a ring set with emeralds and diamonds and there was a bracelet with the same stones too.

At that moment, the sun came out and shone on the bright jewels.

'They are like green fire!' Dorothea exclaimed. She put on the ring and then took it off quickly.

'I shall keep this ring and the bracelet, but I shall not wear them,' she said.

'But how can I wear jewels when you don't?' Celia cried.

'Because we are very different, my dear,' Dorothea said kindly. 'I can't help thinking of the poor people who had to dig these jewels out of the ground. And I like to dress plainly. While women think only of their beauty, no one will ever praise[14] their minds.'

The two sisters had been orphans[15] for more than seven years. Their uncle, Mr Brooke, who had never married, was their guardian[16]. He had sent his nieces to live with good families in England and Switzerland. There they had been taught by governesses[17] until their uncle decided that they were old enough to live with him at Tipton Manor.

Mr Brooke was very fond of Dorothea and Celia and although he knew very little about women, he was happy to look after his nieces.

Two Sisters

Both girls had inherited[18] a little money from their parents. As Dorothea was the elder sister, any future son she might have would inherit Mr Brooke's wealth too. Of course, the Brooke sisters were expected to make good marriages to rich men who owned land and had a big house and many servants. The girls' lives would be spent looking after their husbands and, later on, their children.

Neither of the girls was well-educated. Very few women received a good education in 1829. Yet everyone agreed that Dorothea was clever. She was beautiful too, with long dark hair and large dark eyes. She always dressed very plainly and she wore her hair in an old-fashioned way, but somehow, that only made her look even more lovely.

Dorothea had very strong opinions about many things and she sometimes had strange ideas too. She wanted to use her mind and think for herself, but she also tried to learn as much as she could from other people. She wanted to use her money to make the little world of Middlemarch a better place.

Celia Brooke was very pretty, with light brown hair and brown eyes. She enjoyed wearing fashionable clothes and curling her hair. She was not as serious as her elder sister. But everyone said that Celia was more sensible than the beautiful Dorothea.

Mr Brooke had invited two guests to dinner that evening – the Reverend[19] Mr Casaubon of Lowick Manor, who was a scholar[20], and Sir James Chettam, who lived at Freshitt Hall.

Celia wore the amethysts with her new white dress and she looked very pretty. Dorothea did not wear any jewellery and her dress, as usual, was very plain. But this made her look more beautiful than ever.

Sir James was a handsome young man, who was often a guest at Tipton Grange. Like Mr Brooke, Sir James owned a large estate and a fine house. And, like Mr Brooke, Sir James was a very wealthy man. He had decided that he would ask Dorothea to

Two Sisters

marry him and he was sure that she would say yes. Mr Brooke was fond of his young neighbour and he hoped that Dorothea would agree.

However, Dorothea was not at all interested in Sir James. She believed that he came to Tipton to see her sister, Celia. Dorothea did think of marriage, of course, but not to a young man. Her idea of a husband was an intelligent, older man who would guide her and teach her, like a father.

Dorothea had never met Mr Casaubon before, but she had immediately become interested in his serious conversation. By the side of Sir James, Mr Casaubon looked old and pale. His hair was partly grey and his eyes had deep shadows under them. But Dorothea, listening to the older man's slow careful voice, took no notice of these things.

In answer to a question from Mr Brooke, Mr Casaubon was speaking about his own work.

'I am happy to tell you about it,' he said with a smile. 'I have been studying the subject for many years. In preparation, I have read all the Latin and Greek authors and others too, of course. My aim is to put together all the greatest thoughts on the myths[21] and world religions. I plan to show that they are all part of the same knowledge – of one great plan. My book will be called "The Key to All Mythologies".'

Then Mr Casaubon sighed. 'I still have a great deal of information to put in order before I start writing the book,' he added. 'My health is not always good and I sometimes think that I will die before my work is finished.'

'That would be terrible!' Dorothea said quickly. 'Perhaps you need a secretary to help you arrange your notes. I try to put my uncle's papers in order sometimes, but he won't let me.'

'Well, a woman's mind, you know,' Mr Brooke said with a laugh. 'Women are not trained to do these things, are they, Mr Casaubon?'

When the two girls were alone, after dinner, Celia said,

'How very ugly Mr Casaubon is with his pale face and thin grey hair! He must be at least forty-five years old. He moves his head up and down when he speaks and his voice is so unpleasant.'

'You mustn't talk about Mr Casaubon like that, Celia!' Dorothea cried. 'He is a scholar and he has a very fine mind. I wish that I could help him with his work!'

'To do that, you would have to marry him. What would Sir James Chettam think about that?' Celia replied with a smile.

'Sir James? What do you mean?' Dorothea asked quickly.

'You know what I mean, Dorothea. Sir James wants to marry you,' her sister replied. 'Why do you think that he visits our uncle so often? And why is he so interested in your drawings for the new cottages in Freshitt village? I know that you are very clever, Dorothea, but you don't understand people at all.'

2

Two Letters

Mr Brooke enjoyed talking to Mr Casaubon and he invited him to stay for a short time. Both men were bachelors[22] and when he went to Tipton Grange, Mr Casaubon had no thought of getting married. But before he left, he had several conversations with Dorothea. Mr Casaubon did most of the talking, of course. But Dorothea listened to him with the greatest of pleasure and he was flattered[23] by her attention. Slowly, the idea of sharing his life and work with a lively and interested young woman began to enter Mr Casaubon's mind.

A week or two later, Mr Brooke was invited to Lowick Manor where Mr Casaubon lived. The house was old and rather dark, but the gardens and grounds were very pleasant.

Two Letters

When he returned home, Mr Brooke went into his library and he was pleased to see Dorothea reading there.

'Come nearer the fire, my dear. It is cold today,' Mr Brooke said with a smile. 'I have been to Lowick, you know. I had lunch with Casaubon and had a look at his library too. Lowick is a big house and I think Casaubon is lonely. He needs a companion[24].'

'It would be a great honour[25] for anyone – for any woman – to be that companion,' Dorothea replied.

Her uncle looked at his niece in surprise.

'So you like him then, my dear?' he said. 'Casaubon has a very high opinion of you. A very high opinion,' he repeated slowly.

Dorothea did not reply.

'Well, Casaubon has told me that he wants to marry you,' Mr Brooke said at last. Then he sighed. 'I told him that I had no idea what you thought about that,' he went on. 'Of course, you will marry one day, but he is over forty-five, you know, and his health is not very good. You are not yet twenty. I would have to agree to the marriage. What do you think about it, my dear?'

'If Mr Casaubon makes me an offer, I shall accept him,' Dorothea said in her clear voice. 'I admire and honour[26] him. I am very grateful to Mr Casaubon.'

'Well, he is a wealthy man with a fine estate,' Mr Brooke said. 'I want you to make a good marriage, of course. But Sir James also wants to marry you, you know. He is rich too and much younger than Casaubon.'

'I could never marry Sir James Chettam,' Dorothea said quickly.

Mr Brooke shook his head sadly and sighed again. Women were so difficult to understand.

'I see that you have made up your mind,' he said. 'Well, I have a letter from Casaubon for you. Here it is. Read it carefully and don't answer it until you are sure of your feelings.'

Dorothea took the letter from her uncle and hurried to her room.

Two Letters

The letter was very long, but there was no word of love in it. Edward Casaubon saw Dorothea as a useful companion, someone who would help him complete his life's work. He wrote of his own hopes and said nothing about Dorothea's feelings. But to Dorothea, the letter opened a door to a new world. It was a world where she could do some good and help someone more intelligent than herself. She was happy and proud that this great man had chosen her.

Dorothea sat down at once to answer his letter and her reply was short and clear. She was very grateful and she promised to give her whole life to Mr Casaubon and his work. She rewrote her letter several times until her writing could be read very easily. When she gave the letter to her uncle an hour or so later, he looked at it in some surprise.

'Have you thought enough about this my dear?' he asked in a kind voice.

'There was no need to think. I know my own mind,' Dorothea replied.

Dorothea said nothing to her sister that day, but Celia noticed that Dorothea was looking very happy.

The next day, Mr Brooke received a letter at lunch time.

'It is from Casaubon,' he said to Dorothea. 'He is coming to dinner tonight.'

Celia looked at Dorothea and was very surprised to see that her sister was blushing. For the first time, Celia began to feel suspicious that there was something more between her sister and Mr Casaubon than scholarly conversation.

Later on, when the sisters were in their sitting-room, Celia said, very quietly,

'Is anyone else coming to dinner with Mr Casaubon tonight?'

'No, I don't think so,' Dorothea replied.

'That's a pity,' Celia said with a quiet laugh. 'We shall all hear

Two Letters

him scraping his spoon on his plate when he drinks his soup. He makes such a horrible noise, Dorothea. You must have noticed it.'

Dorothea stood up and walked slowly across the room. Then she turned and looked at her sister.

'Please don't speak about Mr Casaubon like that, Celia,' she said in a clear, serious voice. 'It is right to tell you that I am engaged[27] to be married to him.'

Immediately Celia went very pale and her eyes filled with tears. 'Oh, my dear, I hope that you will be very happy,' she said gently. 'I did not mean to say anything to hurt you. But why Mr Casaubon? How can you think of marrying him?'

'I would ask why can he think of marrying *me*!' Dorothea replied. 'Mr Casaubon has a great mind, Celia, and he has chosen me to help him in his life's work. I had hoped that you would understand.'

'I will try,' Celia promised sadly.

That evening, Dorothea did her best to show Mr Casaubon how happy she was. She listened carefully to every word he said and asked several questions about his work. Mr Casaubon was delighted.

'My dear Miss Brooke – Dorothea,' he said. 'You have all the best qualities of women and you are interested in my ideas too. You will help me complete my great work. And you will complete my life too with your simple trust in me. I thank you.'

And so they were both satisfied. Dorothea wanted to be good enough for Mr Casaubon and he hoped that she would be good enough for him. They both agreed that the marriage would take place in six weeks' time.

The people of Middlemarch were very surprised when they heard the news and everyone thought that it was very strange. All Mr Brooke's friends agreed that he should have stopped Dorothea from taking such an unusual decision.

Sir James Chettam was shocked and angry. 'Why has a boring old bachelor like Casaubon decided to marry at his age?' the young man cried. 'And why has a beautiful young girl like Dorothea Brooke agreed to marry him?'

But Sir James said nothing to Dorothea herself. He went on helping her with the plans for the new cottages in Freshitt village. Whenever Sir James visited Tipton Grange, he slowly began to notice that Celia was much more sensible than her sister. And she was very pretty too.

3

Middlemarch

Middlemarch was a small town in the middle of England. In 1829, when this story begins, England was beginning to change in many ways. But these changes were slow in coming to Middlemarch. The people there preferred the old ways and they did not like change at all.

The manufacturers[28], the tradesmen[29] and the farmers all knew each other and many of them belonged to the same families. They respected wealthy people like the Brookes who owned land and lived in the big houses outside the town, but they gossiped about them too. The people of Middlemarch often laughed at Mr Brooke and his unusual political ideas. They did not understand his niece, Dorothea, either, and her coming marriage to Mr Casaubon surprised them very much. The people of Middlemarch waited to see what would happen next.

Dorothea knew nothing of this gossip as she prepared herself for married life.

One grey November day, Dorothea went with her sister and her uncle to Lowick to see her new home.

'Oh dear!' Celia said to herself, as the carriage stopped outside the house. 'What a dull, dark place Lowick Manor is. Freshitt Hall, where Sir James lives, is much more pleasant.'

But Dorothea was delighted with everything at Lowick Manor. Here she would live as Mr Casaubon's wife. Here, she could be happy and useful. She saw nothing that she wanted to change and that pleased Mr Casaubon very much.

'Perhaps you would like to choose a sitting-room for yourself, my dear,' Mr Casaubon said with a smile and a nod of his head.

'Oh, any room will do,' Dorothea replied. 'You must decide for me.'

'There is a room upstairs,' Celia said quickly. 'It has such a big window, with a lovely view of the gardens.'

Mr Casaubon smiled again and nodded his head. 'A very good choice,' he replied, leading the way. All his visitors followed him upstairs. Mr Casaubon walked along a corridor, opened a door and said quietly,

'This was my mother's room, Dorothea. She was always happy here and I hope you will be too. The furniture is a little old-fashioned now. You can change anything you like.'

'No, it is beautiful,' Dorothea cried. 'I don't want you to waste your money on buying new things for me. I don't want to change anything at all.'

She moved about the room and stopped before some little portraits[30].

'This must be your mother's picture. You have shown me one like it downstairs,' she said. 'And who is this?'

'That is her elder sister, my aunt Julia,' Mr Casaubon answered.

'You have not mentioned her before,' Dorothea said. 'She has an interesting face.'

'It is a very pretty one,' Celia said, 'with those grey eyes and brown curly hair.'

'She made an unfortunate marriage. I never met her,' Casaubon said quietly. 'Why don't we walk in the gardens now?'

They all walked slowly between two lines of trees to the little church where Casaubon preached[31] every Sunday. Then they returned to the house by a different way.

'Who is that young man over there?' Mr Brooke asked. 'He's sketching that tree, I think. Let's go and have a look, my dears.'

He walked towards the tree and the young man who was drawing it. Mr Casaubon did not look very pleased.

'That is my cousin – Mr Will Ladislaw,' Mr Casaubon replied. 'He is the grandson of my aunt Julia. He's staying here at Lowick for a short time.'

The young man stood up as they all walked towards him. He was very handsome, with the same grey eyes and brown curly hair as the portrait.

'Dorothea, let me introduce you to my cousin, Mr Ladislaw,' Casaubon said. 'Will, this is Miss Brooke. I have told you about her. And this is her sister, Celia.'

Will Ladislaw bowed[32] but he did not smile. Instead, he looked at Dorothea coldly. Will had already made up his mind. Any girl who was going to marry his unpleasant cousin, Edward Casaubon, must be unpleasant too, however beautiful she was.

After Mr Casaubon had introduced him to Will Ladislaw, Mr Brooke began chatting in his usual way.

'You are an artist, I see,' he said to Will.

'No, I just draw a little,' the young man replied.

'And so did I, when I was your age,' Mr Brooke said cheerfully. 'I could have been an artist, if I had worked harder. I collected pictures too, when I was on my travels. You must come to my house, Tipton Grange, you know, and look at them. My nieces have never learnt anything about art. They're not interested in

'Dorothea, let me introduce you to my cousin,
Mr Ladislaw,' Casaubon said.

my pictures at all. I would like you to give me your opinion of them.'

'Thank you. I would like to see your pictures,' Will replied.

'I think it is time to get back to the house now,' Casaubon said. 'The young ladies will be tired of standing.'

He walked with his guests towards the house and Will sat down and began sketching again. But after a few moments, he put down his pencil and laughed.

'How strange people are!' he said to himself. 'My cousin Casaubon – who is going to marry that beautiful girl! And Miss Brooke herself, who knows nothing about art and her uncle who thinks he knows so much!'

'What is that young man planning to do with his life?' Brooke asked Casaubon as they walked along. 'He draws well, you know.'

'Will finds it difficult to settle on anything,' Casaubon replied coldly. 'He will not be in Middlemarch for very long. He went to a good school, which I paid for, but he refused to go to an English university. He went to study in Germany instead. I believe that he now wants to go abroad again.' Mr Casaubon sighed. 'I have worked very hard all my life,' he said. 'But Will does not want to follow my example, I'm afraid. I have given him enough money to live on for a year or so. Then we will see.'

'That is very kind of you, and patient too,' Dorothea said with a smile. 'We must all try to be patient with one another, I think. I do hope your cousin will settle down[33] soon.'

But Will Ladislaw was too impatient to stay in Middlemarch any longer. Six days later, he left for Europe and the people of Middlemarch, who did not welcome strangers, soon forgot about him.

In a few weeks, Dorothea Brooke and Mr Edward Casaubon were married and on their way to Rome for their honeymoon[34]. Mr Casaubon very much wanted to look at some old manuscripts[35] in the Vatican[36] Library.

4
Doctor Lydgate

Some time before this, the people of Middlemarch had been gossiping about another young stranger – a good-looking young man with thick, dark hair and dark eyes. He was a doctor and he came from a good family in the north of England. His name was Tertius Lydgate. He was young, poor and ambitious.

Doctor Lydgate had chosen to live and work in Middlemarch for a very good reason. He had studied hard in Paris and London to become a surgeon[37] and he was interested in all the latest medical ideas. Now he wanted to work in a small town where he could use these ideas to help people. He wanted to get to know his patients[38], especially the poor ones.

The people of Middlemarch did not like new ideas, but Dr Lydgate was very sympathetic[39]. He listened to his patients and asked them sensible questions about their illnesses. His ideas seemed strange, but most of his patients got better.

Mr Bulstrode, a rich banker who had lived in Middlemarch for many years, spoke to Mr Brooke about the young doctor.

'Lydgate is an interesting young man,' Bulstrode said. 'I believe that you know his family.'

'Not exactly,' Mr Brooke replied. 'But his uncle, the baronet[40], sent me a letter about him. Lydgate is clever. He studied in Paris, you know. He has lots of new ideas – fresh air, diet, that kind of thing.'

'Middlemarch doctors are very old-fashioned,' Mr Bulstrode said. 'We should welcome Doctor Lydgate to our town. He might be interested in my ideas for the New Hospital. He might like to work there, too. I must speak to him about it.'

Lydgate was soon invited into the homes of several Middlemarch families, including Tipton Grange, where he met

Doctor Lydgate

Dorothea Brooke. She told him her ideas for helping the poor people of the neighbourhood.

'Miss Brooke is a fine-looking girl,' Lydgate said to himself, as he made his way home. 'But she asks too many questions – she is too serious for me. Her ideas are good, but she does not always think clearly. She will be happy with Mr Casaubon, I think. He will be her teacher, as well as her husband.'

Lydgate was also invited to the home of the Vincys, a manufacturing family who lived in the centre of the town. The Vincys were related to nearly all the respectable families in Middlemarch. Mr Vincy's sister was married to Mr Bulstrode, the rich banker. The Vincys were not as rich or as important as the Brookes and they were never invited to Tipton Grange. But the Vincys had always worked hard and they were well-respected in the town.

Rosamond Vincy, their daughter, was the most beautiful girl in Middlemarch. She was tall, with an elegant[41] figure. She had dark blue eyes and pale blonde hair. She had been to a fashionable school, but had learnt little more than how to play the piano, sing and embroider[42] neatly. All the young men in Middlemarch were in love with Rosamond, but she was not interested in any of them.

Rosamond had marriage plans, of course. She planned to marry a rich, ambitious and handsome man from a good family who would admire her beauty and give her everything that she wanted.

'How can I find that young man in Middlemarch?' Rosamond would ask herself, with a sigh.

But when Doctor Lydgate came to live in the town, Rosamond Vincy thought she had found her perfect husband and she soon found out all she could about him.

'I'd like to know Doctor Lydgate. You must ask him to dinner, Mamma,' Rosamond told her mother. 'Dr Lydgate is very clever – everyone says so – and his uncle is a baronet too.'

Doctor Lydgate

'He sounds like an interesting young man,' Mrs Vincy said with a smile. 'I think that we would all like to meet him.'

And so Tertius Lydgate met Rosamond Vincy.

Rosamond knew the power of her own beauty. She was not surprised to see the look of admiration on the young doctor's face when he saw her for the first time. They sat next to each other at dinner and were soon talking happily together.

'How lovely she is,' he said to himself. And to Rosamond he added, 'You will let me hear you play the piano tonight, I hope. And you will sing too, perhaps.'

Rosamond smiled. 'That will stop my brother Fred from trying to play,' she said. 'He is a very bad musician indeed.'

Fred Vincy was sitting on the other side of the table.

'Thank you, Rosy' he said. 'I suppose you will tell Lydgate that I am a bad scholar too.'

'Well, you left Oxford without taking your degree[43],' Rosamond said. 'What are your plans now?'

'I shall go back to my college and this time, I'll work hard and get my degree,' Fred replied. 'Mary Garth will never forgive me if I don't.'

'Who's Mary Garth?' Lydgate asked Rosamond quietly.

Rosamond turned her head gracefully and smiled.

'The Garths are a farming family,' she replied. 'They are rather poor, so Mary has to work. She is a dear girl and a very good friend of mine, but no one can say that she's beautiful. Mary is short and plain, but my handsome, lazy brother says that he loves her.'

'And so I do!' Fred Vincy said. 'I have loved her all my life and I think she loves me too. Mary Garth is sensible and good-natured, which is better than being beautiful, Rosy!'

Rosamond laughed. 'I am not sure about that!' she said, 'but she certainly has to work hard. And only a good-natured girl could look after our Uncle Peter – Mr Peter Featherstone. Mary is the housekeeper at Stone Court, where he lives.'

'I don't think that I have met Mr Featherstone,' Lydgate said.

Doctor Lydgate

'He is old and very ill,' Rosamond explained, 'So you may be called to Stone Court any day soon, Doctor Lydgate. But be careful! Uncle Peter is very bad-tempered, isn't he, Fred?'

'And very rich too,' Fred replied. 'I hope that he leaves us a lot of money when he dies. I go to Stone Court to see him when I can.'

'And to see Mary Garth too,' his sister said and her brother laughed.

After dinner, Rosamond played the piano as she had promised. Lydgate was very fond of music and his admiration for the beautiful girl grew with every note she played. She sang too and by the end of the evening Lydgate was very happy that he had decided to live in Middlemarch.

As Rosamond sat down beside him again, she said,

'Do you dance, Dr Lydgate? Or perhaps clever men like you never dance.'

'I would be happy to dance with you, Miss Vincy,' Lydgate said.

Rosamond laughed. 'We do sometimes have dancing in the evenings,' she said. 'I wasn't sure if you would come or not.'

'I would come if you would be my partner,' Lydgate replied. 'That would make me very happy.'

Rosamond smiled. She had already made up her mind to marry the handsome young doctor and, as she was used to getting her own way[44], she was sure that she would succeed.

On his way home, Lydgate thought of Rosamond Vincy. He felt quite safe from her charm[45] and her beauty. Though he believed that Rosamond Vincy would make someone the perfect wife, Lydgate knew that he could not afford to marry for several years. At the moment he had more important plans, like looking into new research on cholera[46], a subject that he was very interested in. Lydgate loved his work and the development of his skills as a doctor was the most important thing in his life.

For Rosamond, the evening had a different meaning. She had chosen Tertius Lydgate to be her husband. She remembered every look and word of his throughout the evening. She was sure that he was in love with her. He was handsome and clever and best of all, the young doctor came from a good family. His uncle was a baronet.

'When I am married to Tertius, I will take my place in the very best Middlemarch society,' Rosamond thought to herself. 'When Tertius is rich and famous, everyone will forget that I used to be Rosamond Vincy, whose father was only a manufacturer.'

It was true that Tertius Lydgate was not rich yet, but he was very ambitious. Rosamond was sure that he would be very successful. As the clever young doctor's elegant and beautiful wife, Rosamond would be admired by society and their lives together would be very happy.

These were Rosamond's dreams and she was determined to make them come true.

So the beautiful girl played the piano and sang happily and took care always to look her best. She read romantic novels and poems about love and prepared for a perfect future with a perfect husband.

5

A Meeting in Rome

Mr and Mrs Casaubon had been in Rome for five weeks. Mrs Casaubon – Dorothea – was alone in their apartment and she was crying.

Why was Dorothea so unhappy, that afternoon in Rome? She had not been forced into marriage. Indeed, several people

A Meeting in Rome

had tried to stop her marrying Mr Casaubon. But Dorothea had believed that she could help her husband finish his great work. She hoped that her dedication[47] and youthful enthusiasm[48] would play a part in her husband's final success.

But that morning, she had learnt the truth and it had made her very unhappy.

'I hope that you are satisfied with your time here in Rome,' Dorothea had said to her husband at breakfast.

'Well, yes,' he answered slowly. 'There is more material[49] here than I thought and it has been hard work to take so many notes. But your company has helped me a little.'

Dorothea's eyes had filled with angry tears.

'I am glad that my presence has helped you *a little*,' she said. 'I had hoped that I could do more for you. You have many books full of notes at Lowick – too many perhaps. When we return home, you should decide what to use when you finally write your great book. Surely I can help you with that. You can dictate[50] your final notes to me and I shall write them down. In that way, I shall be really helping you.'

Mr Casaubon's pale face went red with anger. He was used to praise from his young wife, not criticism.

'My love,' Casaubon replied quickly and angrily, 'you are not a scholar and you have little or no knowledge of my work. You are only a woman, after all, with a woman's inferior mind. You have no right to judge me.'

Now Dorothea was angry too.

'You have shown me all your notebooks,' she said. 'But you have never discussed your work with me or talked about writing your book. That is all I know. I am not judging you. I only want to help you.'

Mr Causabon did not reply and Dorothea walked out of the room. But when her husband drove to the Vatican as usual, Dorothea went with him. She spent an hour in the museum there

A Meeting in Rome

before taking the carriage back to their apartment. As she drove through the crowded streets with her maid, Dorothea thought how little she knew about the people of the great city of Rome and how lonely she was there.

When Dorothea was in her own bedroom again, she had cried and cried.

In the afternoon, there was a knock at the door of the room and Dorothea dried her eyes quickly.

'What is it, Tantripp?' Dorothea asked as her maid came into the room.

'There's a gentleman waiting downstairs,' Tantripp replied. 'He says he is a relation of Mr Casaubon's. He gave me his card. Will you see him, Madam?'

Dorothea looked at the card quickly.

'Yes,' she said. 'Please tell Mr Ladislaw to come up. I'll see him in the large sitting-room.'

Dorothea greeted Will with her sweetest smile and held out her hand. The young man could see that she had been crying and at once he felt sorry for her.

'I saw you this morning in the Vatican Museum,' Will said quickly. 'I did not know that you and Mr Casaubon were in Rome. I found out your address and came to visit you both. I am sorry that my cousin is not here.'

'I'm afraid that my husband spends the whole day, from breakfast to dinner, in the Vatican Library,' Dorothea replied. 'He is working very hard, because we shall be leaving Rome soon.'

Will did not know whether to laugh or cry. His boring old cousin had married this beautiful girl, then he left her alone all day!

After a moment, Will smiled and Dorothea smiled back.

'There are so many beautiful things to see in Rome,' Will said. 'I wish there was time to show them to you. But perhaps you are not as fond of art as your uncle is.'

'I do not understand it,' Dorothea said, like a child. 'There are so many paintings here in Rome that I have become confused by them all. But you are an artist, I believe, Mr Ladislaw.'

'I am not good enough to make art my profession[51],' Will explained. 'And, in any case, I am soon going to leave Rome and return to England. Your husband has been generous, but it is time I found work for myself. I don't yet know what that work will be. I find many things of interest, but I find it difficult to choose what would be best for me.'

'You need more patience, perhaps,' Dorothea said gently. 'That's what my husband says.'

'I know what my cousin thinks about me,' Will replied. 'He and I are different in many ways.'

'I agree. Not many men work as hard as Mr Casaubon does,' Dorothea said proudly.

'Let us hope that his work will not, in the end, be useless,' Will said. 'Mr Casaubon does not know German, I believe. If he did, it would have saved him a lot of trouble. All the most modern work on his subject has been written by German scholars and they have many new ideas that Mr Casaubon knows nothing about.'

As she listened, Dorothea felt a strong fear that all her husband's work might have been a waste of time.

'Oh, dear,' Dorothea said sadly. 'I don't know German either. Why didn't I learn it when Celia and I were living in Switzerland? Then I could be of more use to my husband now.'

Will Ladislaw was still thinking about Dorothea's words when Edward Casaubon came into the room.

The two men looked very different – one was old and grey, the other young, lively and good-natured. Casaubon bowed politely. He was not pleased to see his cousin alone with Dorothea. Will was quick to understand this and he soon left.

Casaubon sat down slowly and rested his head on his hand.

'You are tired,' Dorothea said gently. 'I'm afraid I upset you this morning and I'm sorry.'

Home Again

'I am glad that you feel like that, my dear,' Casaubon said.

'Then do you forgive me?' Dorothea asked, sitting down beside her husband.

'Your sorrow is enough,' he replied. 'I am too tired to say any more now.'

'Then I shall give you some good news. It's about your cousin Will,' Dorothea said.

'What is it, my love?' Casaubon asked coldly.

'Will has decided to stop travelling in Europe,' Dorothea replied with a happy smile. 'He is going back to England, to find work and to settle down. He has been grateful for your generosity, of course. But he feels now that he must do without it. He said he would write to you.'

'Oh, did he?' Casaubon said with an unpleasant smile. 'I wonder exactly what work he is thinking of and who will pay him for doing it. I did my duty, that is all. I have no further interest in that young man, my dear. I do not want you to mention his name again.'

Edward Casaubon had very few strong feelings, but jealousy of his young cousin was one of them. And this jealousy, though Casaubon kept it hidden, was growing in his heart, day by day.

6

Home Again

Mr and Mrs Casaubon had arrived back at Lowick Manor in the middle of February. Now Dorothea was standing at the window of her sitting-room. She was looking at the snow as it fell gently onto the garden. Dorothea sighed. Then she turned to look at the room and she remembered the first time that she had seen it. She had thought that it was a very pretty room. Nearly three

Home Again

months had passed since then and now it looked a sad, lonely place.

Then Dorothea saw the little portrait of Will Ladislaw's grandmother and sighed again. The face was strong, but it was unhappy too.

'That poor woman's marriage was a mistake,' Dorothea thought to herself sadly. 'Is my marriage a mistake too? I must speak to my husband again. I must tell him how much I want to help him!'

Dorothea hurried out of the room. But when she reached the top of the dark stairs, she saw Celia coming towards her and she held out her arms to welcome her sister. Mr Brooke was down in the hall, talking to Mr Casaubon.

Dorothea was delighted to see her pretty sister again. After Dorothea had greeted her uncle, the sisters went into Dorothea's room and sat down together by the fire.

'Tell me about Rome, Dorothea dear,' Celia said, holding her sister's hand in her own. 'What did you do there? Is it a nice place to go for a honeymoon?' she added with a soft laugh.

Dorothea looked surprised.

'I... I don't think that it would suit you, dear. But why do you ask?' she said. Then she saw that Celia was blushing and smiling.

'Celia! Has something happened? Have you got some news for me?' Dorothea asked quickly.

Celia laughed again. 'Well, you were away, dear and he – Sir James – had no one else to talk to. Three days ago, he asked me to marry him. Oh, I am so happy!' Celia cried. 'I so enjoy being engaged. Are you pleased too, dear, or do you only like very clever men, now?'

'How can you say that, Celia!' Dorothea replied with a smile. 'Of course I am pleased for you. Sir James is a kind man and he will make you a very good husband. Cleverness is not always important.'

Dorothea was actually a little tired of clever men, but she did not say so.

Home Again

Some weeks later, Dorothea was sitting in the library with her husband. She could see that something had annoyed him and at last he said,

'Dorothea, here is a letter for you. It was with a letter sent to me.'

Dorothea took the letter and smiled.

'It is from Mr Ladislaw,' she said. 'Why is he writing to me?'

'I do not know. But in his letter to me, he suggests visiting Lowick Manor for a time. That will not be possible. Guests tire me and they stop me getting on with my work. I find my cousin Will especially annoying, however much you enjoy his company, my dear.'

Dorothea and Casaubon had not argued since that day in Rome. She had found it was easier to keep quiet rather than show her annoyance. But at hearing these words, she suddenly became very angry.

'Why do you think that I want to annoy you?' she cried. 'How do you know what I think about Will Ladislaw? When have I ever put my own pleasure before yours?'

Mr Casaubon was very surprised by Dorothea's words.

'Please think about what you are saying,' he said nervously.

'I could say the same thing to you!' Dorothea replied.

She waited, expecting her husband to apologize. But Mr Casaubon, his voice shaking, said,

'I do not wish to hear any more about this. Arguments tire me.'

He tried to go on writing, but his hand was shaking so much that he could not hold his pen.

Dorothea left both letters on her husband's desk and sat down at her own table. She worked calmly. Her hand did not shake. It was very steady as she copied the notes that Casaubon had given her the day before.

Her husband was standing now. He was holding on to his desk, unable to breathe and his face was grey.

Home Again

They worked in silence for half an hour. Then a book fell to the floor with a loud noise. Dorothea looked up. Her husband was standing now. He was holding on to his desk, unable to breathe and his face was grey.

Dorothea ran towards him. 'Let me help you. Hold on to me,' she said quietly. She rang the bell for a servant and they helped Mr Casaubon to a couch[52].

Then Sir James Chettam, who was visiting Lowick with Celia, came through the open door. He immediately saw what was happening.

'Mr Casaubon needs help and he needs it quickly,' Sir James said. 'We must send a servant to find Lydgate at once. He is the best doctor in Middlemarch.'

Dorothea looked at her husband and he nodded.

When the servant had left, Sir James went into the sitting-room, to tell Celia what had happened.

'Poor dear Dorothea! How terrible for her!' Celia cried. 'I know that it is very sad and shocking that Mr Casaubon is ill, but I have never liked him. I don't think that he loves Dorothea at all!'

'Why on earth[53] did your sister marry a man like that?' Sir James asked. 'I cannot believe that she loves him. The marriage was wrong, very wrong! Why did your uncle allow it?'

'Poor Dorothea. She never does what other people do. She never has and she never will,' Celia said sadly.

'She has a good heart,' Sir James replied. 'But it is sometimes a foolish[54] one too.'

'Shall I go and see her?' Celia asked. 'Do you think that I could help her?'

'I am sure you could,' Sir James said kindly. 'See her for a few minutes before Lydgate comes. Don't stay long. This has all been a great shock for her.'

Home Again

Lydgate paid several visits to Lowick Manor in the next two weeks. He was interested in studying Mr Casaubon's case[55]. But Dorothea interested Lydgate too and he decided to talk to her. She had to know the truth about her husband's illness.

The library had been shut up for some time, but Dorothea asked Lydgate to see her there.

'I hope Mr Casaubon will soon be able to work here again,' Dorothea said. 'He is a little better, isn't he? Please be honest with me, Dr Lydgate. Do you think my husband's illness will return?'

Dr Lydgate was silent for a few moments. Then he said,

'You must be sure that he does not study too hard or worry too much about his work. Mr Casaubon may live for another fifteen years if...'

'If we are very careful,' Dorothea said slowly.

'Yes, he must not over-work. And anxiety[56] of any kind will be bad for him,' Lydgate replied.

'Oh, you must advise me!' Dorothea cried. 'How can I help him? I so want to help him! His work is his life. He cares for nothing else and neither do I!'

'You can help your husband by staying calm too,' Lydgate replied. 'And please be sure that nothing happens to upset him.'

When Lydgate had left, Dorothea began to cry and cry. She felt that she was to blame for her husband's illness.

'Will's letters upset him very much,' she said to herself. 'I did not understand how angry poor Edward was. I spoke without thinking and that made him even more angry. I must read through the letters quickly and then put them away. I shall ask my uncle to write to Will Ladislaw. He cannot come here again. Perhaps it would be better if Will stayed away from Middlemarch altogether. I wonder why Edward dislikes him so much.'

Mr Brooke did as Dorothea asked. In his letter to Will, Mr Brooke told the young man that Mr Casaubon was ill and so there could be no visitors at Lowick. But Mr Brooke was interested in

Will Ladislaw. Without telling Dorothea, her uncle invited Will to stay at Tipton Grange with him.

'Celia will be married soon and then I shall be lonely,' Mr Brooke thought. 'I enjoy talking to young Ladislaw. If I go into politics one day, Will Ladislaw could help me write speeches and so on. He is full of good ideas.'

When Lydgate next spent an evening at the Vincys, Rosamond asked him about the Casaubons.

'All Mrs Casaubon's thoughts are for her husband,' Lydgate said. 'She must love him, I suppose. It is strange, because Mr Casaubon is more than twice her age.'

'What does his age matter? Of course Mrs Casaubon loves her husband! All wives love their husbands, don't they?' Rosamond cried. 'People say she is very good looking,' she added. 'Did you think she was beautiful?'

'I haven't thought about it,' Lydgate replied, and Rosamond smiled.

7

An Engagement

Fred and Rosamond Vincy's uncle, Peter Featherstone, was now very ill. The two young people were sure that when Mr Featherstone died, he would leave them a great deal of money in his will[57].

Mr Lydgate was the old man's doctor now. Mr Featherstone hated being ill and he behaved very badly. He was rude and bad-tempered to everyone, even Mary Garth, who was very patient with him.

An Engagement

'I hate the way that my uncle speaks to you,' Fred Vincy said to Mary Garth one day. 'The old man treats you like a servant.'

Mary laughed and her plain face looked almost pretty.

'I *am* his servant,' she replied. 'We must never forget that, Fred. I am here because I need the money to help my family.'

'One day soon, I'll have more than enough money for us both,' Fred answered. 'Then my Mary will be a fine lady!'

But Mary shook her head.

'I'll never be a fine lady, but I hope that I'll always be your Mary,' she said quietly. 'Money will never change me and I hope it won't change you either, Fred. But don't be too sure that you know what Mr Featherstone has decided. No one knows what his plans are.'

Meanwhile, Rosamond went on making plans for her own future. Everyone in Middlemarch agreed that Rosamond Vincy was sweet and charming. She had always been spoilt and she was used to getting her own way in everything. Many men in Middlemarch had fallen in love with her and she was used to turning their offers down[58]. Now the beautiful young girl had made up her mind to marry Tertius Lydgate and she could not believe that he would refuse her.

The people of Middlemarch soon began to gossip about the amount of time that Rosamond and the doctor were spending together. Mrs Bulstrode decided to speak to Rosamond about it.

'I am your aunt, your father's sister, and yet I have not been told the news,' she said to her niece one day.

'What news, aunt?' Rosamond asked quietly.

'The news about your engagement, of course,' Mrs Bulstrode replied. 'Your engagement to young Dr Lydgate!'

Rosamond blushed deeply and she turned her head away.

'I am not engaged, aunt,' she said quietly.

'Well, everyone in Middlemarch thinks you are!' Mrs Bulstrode exclaimed.

An Engagement

'I don't care what Middlemarch thinks,' Rosamond replied, with a smile. But she was secretly rather pleased that people had been talking about her.

'Oh, you should care, my dear,' Mrs Bulstrode said. 'Dr Lydgate is very clever, but he is not a rich man. And your father has no money to give you. You could never be happy if you were married to a poor man.'

'Mr Lydgate is not a poor man, aunt,' Rosamond replied. 'He comes from a very good family. His uncle is a baronet who lives in a big house in the north of England. He has plenty of money.'

'Dr Lydgate's family may be rich, but he is poor. He told me so himself,' Mrs Bulstrode said. 'Has he asked you to marry him?'

'I would rather not answer that,' Rosamond said quietly. She had not questioned Lydgate's feelings for her before now, and she did not like being unable to say 'Yes'.

When she got home, Mrs Bulstrode spoke to her husband.

'Now that Dr Lydgate is helping you with the New Hospital, you see him nearly every day,' she said. 'You must ask that young man if he is planning to marry Rosamond. Then I will speak to him myself.'

Lydgate's answer was quite clear. He told Mr Bulstrode that he had no intention of marrying at the present time.

Mrs Bulstrode soon found an opportunity to speak to the young doctor herself.

'Young people have to be so careful these days,' she said with a smile. 'Girls, especially pretty ones, must think of the future,' she went on. 'Every girl owes it to her family and to herself to make a good marriage. To marry a poor man is always a great mistake.'

'Of course,' Lydgate answered in some surprise. 'A poor man who was honest would never think of marriage. But that does not stop someone like me from talking to pretty girls. I cannot believe that they will all fall in love with me!' he added.

'Do not be too sure, Mr Lydgate,' Mrs Bulstrode replied.

An Engagement

Lydgate understood the warning. He realized that he had been seeing too much of Rosamond Vincy and that people in Middlemarch were gossiping about them.

'I will not go to the Vincys again, unless I have business with Mr Vincy,' the young man said to himself. 'I am sure that Rosamond will understand. We enjoy each others' company, but we are only friends, after all.'

Ten days went by and, during that time, Doctor Lydgate stayed away from the Vincys' house. Rosamond became very unhappy. She had been dreaming of marriage to Lydgate for the last six months and she could not believe that he had forgotten her so soon.

On the eleventh day, there was a change in Peter Featherstone's health. Dr Lydgate was called to Stone Court, where Mrs Vincy was now helping to look after her brother.

'Please tell my husband the sad news about Mr Featherstone,' she said to the doctor, as he was leaving.

'Of course,' he replied. 'I shall go to the house and leave the message with Rosamond,'

'It will be pleasant to see her again, just for a moment,' Lydgate thought to himself as he rode his horse back into Middlemarch.

When Lydgate came into the room, Rosamond blushed deeply. The doctor gave her his message quickly and then sat there, in silence. Rosamond was sewing and she did not raise her eyes from her embroidery.

At last, Lydgate stood up. He moved so suddenly, that Rosamond dropped her embroidery as she stood up too. Lydgate picked it up quickly and held it out to her. As he looked at Rosamond, he saw the tears which were falling from her large blue eyes and running down her pale face.

'What's the matter? Something has upset you! What is it?' Lydgate cried. Then he put his arms around her and kissed her gently.

A Funeral and a Will

When he left the house half-an-hour later, Lydgate found that somehow, he had become engaged to the beautiful Rosamond.

He called again later that evening, to speak to her father. Mr Vincy was sure that old Mr Featherstone would soon be dead and that he would leave the family enough money to allow Rosamond to marry her handsome young doctor. So her father agreed to the engagement and everything was settled in very few words.

8
A Funeral and a Will

Old Peter Featherstone died, as everyone had expected, and he was buried on a morning in May. The old man had been related to many Middlemarch families and the churchyard at Lowick was full of the people who had come to the old man's funeral. Everyone was dressed in black and many were crying.

Dorothea and the Chettams – Celia was now married to Sir James – watched from an upper window of Lowick Manor. Dorothea looked down at the people of Middlemarch and sighed. They were almost as far away from her own little world as the people of Rome had been.

'It's so strange,' Dorothea said to her sister. 'We live so near these tradesmen and farming people, but we never speak to them. I visit the poor villagers in their cottages nearly every day, but I don't know the people of Middlemarch at all.'

'They all look so unhappy in their black clothes,' Celia replied. 'They are making me feel sad too.'

At that moment, her uncle, Mr Brooke, came into the room.

'Casaubon is back in the library, my dear,' he said to Dorothea. 'He should not be working at his books so soon. I told him to come

A Funeral and a Will

up here and join us. Ah, here he is! I have some news – some good news, you know, my dear.'

Dorothea watched her husband enter and sit down quietly at the back at the room. At that moment, Celia gave a cry of surprise.

'I can see Mr Ladislaw down there,' she said. 'You did not tell me that he had come back, Dorothea!'

Dorothea went very pale.

'But I didn't... Where...?' she began, looking at her husband.

Mr Brooke smiled happily. 'I brought young Ladislaw back here to Middlemarch,' he explained. 'He is staying at the Grange with me. That young man is a credit[59] to you, Casaubon,' Mr Brooke went on in his cheerful way. 'I invited him when you were ill, you know. Dorothea told me he couldn't stay with you and she asked me to write to him.'

Poor Dorothea did not know what to say or do.

'You are very kind, dear sir,' Mr Casaubon said coldly. 'I am sure that my young cousin is most grateful to you.'

'I knew that you would be pleased,' Mr Brooke replied. 'I'll go and fetch him up now!'

The day after the funeral, the members of Peter Featherstone's family came together at Stone Court to hear the lawyer[60] read the old man's will. Most of them lived in Middlemarch, but some of them had come from other towns and villages nearby.

Everyone had hoped that Mr Featherstone would leave them some money, but nearly everyone in the room was disappointed. Fred Vincy, who had thought that he was his uncle's heir[61], was not left anything at all. His mother, Mrs Vincy, was given one hundred pounds and Rosamond was left the same amount.

'The heir to Mr Featherstone's land and property is Mr Joshua Rigg,' the lawyer said in a clear voice, 'He will be living here at Stone Court, and he will take the name of Featherstone.'

A Funeral and a Will

A thin young man coughed and stepped forward. There was a smile on his face, but he did not look surprised. Everyone in the room turned to look at him.

'Why did Peter Featherstone leave all his money to this stranger?' everyone asked themselves. 'Who is he? Why didn't we know about him?'

The young man spoke to no one but the lawyer. But the people of Middlemarch soon found out who Joshua Rigg Featherstone was. He was Peter Featherstone's only son and the old man had kept him a secret from everyone.

The Vincys were all shocked and disappointed by the old man's will. Fred Vincy looked very pale as he walked from the room.

'Never mind, Fred,' Mary Garth said to him kindly. 'I do truly think that you will be better without the money.'

'How can you say that, Mary?' Fred answered angrily. 'I expected the money and I need it too. What can I do now?'

'You know what you must do, my boy,' his father said angrily. 'You must go back to college next term, get your degree and then you can become a clergyman[62]. That's the only job you will be able to do. I have no more money to spare for you now.'

'And if I get my degree what will happen then?' Fred asked. 'I shall have to be a poor clergyman all my life. I shall never have any money to marry!'

'Think of me too, Fred,' Mary Garth said quietly. 'I don't have a job now and I need to work. Go back to college and get your degree and then you can think of the future. You must find a job and live a useful life. But don't become a clergyman, Fred. You would make a very bad one and I could never think of marrying you.'

'Don't talk about marrying, Mary!' Mr Vincy said angrily. 'Marriage is a very expensive business.' Then he turned to Fred. 'Why did your sister Rosy have to get herself engaged to a poor young doctor?' Mr Vincy asked. 'She could have made a better

A Funeral and a Will

marriage than that. I've got no money to pay for wedding-clothes. They will have to wait, that's all. In fact, it would be better if the engagement was ended altogether.'

'Now, I am sure you do not mean that, my dear,' Mrs Vincy said quietly.

'Yes, I do!' her husband replied. 'When I agreed to the marriage, I expected old Featherstone to leave our family a great deal of money. You'd better tell Rosy what I think about her engagement now.'

Mrs Vincy did not reply, but the next morning she spoke to Rosamond and told her what her father had said.

Rosamond smiled and shook her beautiful head gracefully. 'Papa does not mean that,' she said calmly. 'He has always wanted me to marry for love. Well, I love Dr Lydgate and I shall marry him. Papa gave his consent seven weeks ago. He can't change his mind now.

'Old Mrs Bretton's house is empty and we can rent that,' Rosamond went on. 'It is a good house, in the best part of Middlemarch. Tertius and I will be happy there. We shall need new carpets and furniture, of course. Everything must be the very best. I know that Tertius will want that.'

Rosamond was right. Lydgate was used to having the best of everything and he had no wish to live like a poor man. After all, his family was a good one – far better than the Vincys. Lydgate felt that the sooner that he and his bride were living in their own home, the better.

One evening, a week or two later, Lydgate went to the Vincys' house and found Rosamond there alone.

'My dearest, you have been crying,' he said gently. 'Something has upset you. What is the matter? Please tell me.'

Rosamond sighed deeply. 'Papa has been so bad-tempered recently,' she said sadly. 'This morning, he had an argument with Fred. It was about money, of course. And I feel that Papa is not

A Funeral and a Will

quite pleased about our engagement,' she added, very quietly. 'He said that I should speak to you about... about... giving it up.'

'Will you give it up?' Lydgate cried.

'No, I never give up anything that I want,' Rosamond answered calmly.

'Thank God!' Lydgate said. 'You are over twenty-one. Your father cannot stop the marriage. In fact, now we have the house, I would like us to be married as soon as possible. Let's say in six weeks' time, dearest.'

Rosamond turned her neck gracefully and smoothed down her fair hair with her little white hand.

'Then write to Papa, Tertius,' she said with a smile. 'Tell him our plans, so that he can agree to them.'

The next day, Rosamond walked with her father to his warehouse[63]. She told him that Lydgate wanted the marriage to take place soon.

'Nonsense, my dear,' Mr Vincy said. 'You are the most beautiful girl in Middlemarch and I have spent a lot of money on preparing you to make a good marriage. Why must you throw yourself away on a poor man?'

'Mr Lydgate will be rich very soon, Papa,' Rosamond replied. 'The Casaubons and the Chettams have chosen him as their doctor. You know that Tertius comes from a very good family and he is clever too. I am sure that he will make a great scientific discovery, one day. He will find a way of preventing cholera, perhaps. Then he will be very famous.'

Mr Vincy was silent.

'I cannot give up my only hope of happiness, Papa,' Rosamond went on. 'Mr Lydgate is a gentleman. I could not love him if he was not. He is the perfect husband for me. You don't want me to become ill, do you, Papa? You know that I never change my mind. I will be very ill, if you try to stop my marriage to Tertius Lydgate.'

'Well, well, child. Tell him to write to me and I will give him an answer,' Mr Vincy said at last and his daughter smiled.

In his answer, Mr Vincy asked Lydgate to insure[64] his life to protect Rosamond's future and Lydgate agreed. That satisfied Mr Vincy and the preparations for the marriage went on.

'I think that you should write to your uncle, Sir Godwin,' Rosamond said to Lydgate one day. 'Tell him that we will visit him on our honeymoon.'

'And perhaps he will give you some money,' Mrs Vincy added cheerfully. 'A baronet could easily spare you two thousand pounds, I am sure!'

Lydgate said nothing, but he looked unhappy. Rosamond was angry with her mother and the girl decided that persuading Tertius to leave Middlemarch in a year or two, would be a very good idea.

'We would both be happier in London,' Rosamond said to herself. 'Tertius would soon become famous if we were living there and we would be meeting people from the very best society.'

But Rosamond did not talk to Lydgate about this idea.

9

The Cousins

Mr Brooke had become very interested in politics. He had bought a local radical[65] newspaper called the *Pioneer*[66] and planned to use it to tell people about his ideas and the need for reform.

'The people of Middlemarch live in the past.' Mr Brooke said to Sir James Chettam one day. 'I want to interest them in new ideas – ideas that have changed the future in other countries. They could change the future here too.'

The Cousins

'The old ideas are the best for England,' Sir James replied. 'We both belong to good old families. We both own land and have many people working for us. We must look after them in the old ways. People who live in the countryside or in small towns like Middlemarch do not like change.'

But Mr Brooke did not agree with Sir James.

'My newspaper will explain everything,' he said. 'I will show the people here that change will come, whether they like it or not. Factories are being built and soon we shall have a railway. And, of course, Parliament must be reformed. That is the most important thing, you know.'

Mr Brooke also discussed his ideas with Will Ladislaw, who agreed with most of them.

'I can talk well, but I am not good at writing my ideas down,' Mr Brooke told the young man. 'I would like you to explain these ideas in my newspaper. Will you help me? Stay here at Tipton Grange and we can work together!'

Soon Will was writing many of the articles[67] in Mr Brooke's own newspaper. Mr Brooke was delighted with the young man and he told Mr Casaubon so.

'Your cousin is a fine young man,' Mr Brooke said. 'He has good ideas, you know, and we work together very well. Good writing is a family skill, Casaubon. You must be proud of Will and I am sure you are pleased that he is staying at the Grange with me.'

Mr Brooke, of course, had no idea what Casaubon thought about Will and he had no idea how much the older man hated his young cousin. Casaubon had hated Will when he was helping him. He hated him even more, now that Will no longer needed him. Casaubon wished that Will would go far away from Middlemarch and he made sure that the young man was never invited to Lowick Manor.

Will understood his cousin's feelings about him very well. He also thought that Casaubon had been very wrong to marry

The Cousins

Dorothea Brooke. Will had become very interested in Casaubon's beautiful young wife. He always enjoyed talking to her, but they did not often have the chance to see each other alone.

One day, Will decided that he wanted to make a sketch of some trees at Lowick. He sat down in a place where Dorothea liked to walk and began to draw. But almost at once, clouds covered the sky and heavy rain began to fall. Will ran into the house where he met the butler[68] in the hall.

'Don't announce me, Pratt,' Will said quickly. 'I know that Mr Casaubon does not like to be disturbed.'

'Mr Casaubon is out, sir,' Pratt answered. 'But Mrs Casaubon is in the library. I'll tell her that you are here, sir, shall I?'

'Oh, very well,' Will said. 'It's raining really hard now. I must give up sketching for the day.'

In another minute, he was in the library, where Dorothea greeted him with her sweetest smile.

'I am so glad that you have come,' she said. 'I am afraid Mr Casaubon will be out all day. Did you want to see him about something?'

'No, no,' Will said quickly. 'I came to sketch, but the rain drove me inside.'

'Then I am pleased that it is raining,' Dorothea replied.

She felt that Will's visit was like a window opening and letting the light into a darkened room.

'We have not been alone since Rome.' Will said quietly.

'I have been studying a great deal since then,' Dorothea said. 'I can read and understand Greek and Latin a little now. I am trying so hard to help my husband, you see. A woman can do nothing by herself, so my plan is to spend my life making his work easier.'

'Perhaps you are working too hard,' Will replied. 'You look very pale. You stay indoors too much. Mr Casaubon should get a secretary.'

The Cousins

'But what would I do then?' poor Dorothea cried. 'The villagers of Lowick have everything that they need. There is nothing for me to do here. I want to help my husband more, not less. He would hate to have a secretary!'

'Mr Casaubon offered me that job once,' Will said with a smile, 'but I was not good enough for it.'

Dorothea smiled. 'You were not a steady worker,' she said.

'That is not true,' Will answered. 'Mr Casaubon may have told you that, but the truth is, he does not like anyone to criticise his work. He is too unsure of himself. I disagreed with his ideas. That was the problem. And that is why he dislikes me.'

Dorothea did not answer at once. Then she said,

'Mr Casaubon has helped you, in spite of his feelings. He must be praised for that.'

'Of course,' Will said quickly. 'He has been very fair. My grandmother was disinherited[69] because she left her family to marry a poor man – a Polish refugee[70]. They were happy together, I think, but they both died very young.'

'I wish that I had known her!' Dorothea cried. 'It must have been so difficult to be poor, after being so rich! She must have loved her husband so much, to give up everything for him. Do you know anything more about them?'

'They both died before I was born,' Will said. 'My grandfather was a clever man – he was musical and he spoke several languages. My father was musical too and of course, he was very poor.'

'It's a different world,' Dorothea said, looking sadly at Will with her beautiful dark eyes. 'I have always had too much of everything. I cannot imagine being poor. But how did Mr Casaubon…?'

'My father wrote to him to ask for help,' Will explained. 'I remember being hungry and my father was very ill by then. He died very soon afterwards and Mr Casaubon took care of my mother and myself.'

'And is your mother still alive?' Dorothea asked quietly.

The Cousins

'No, she died four years ago. She had a difficult life. When she was young, she had left her family too – but for a different reason. She was very pretty and she ran away to become an actress. So you see, if I am a rebel, it is in my blood,' Will added with a smile. 'But I never wish to do anything that you would not approve of.'

'That is very good of you,' Dorothea said with a laugh. 'But I expect you will be leaving the Grange soon. You will get tired of your friends in Middlemarch.'

'That is not true,' Will replied. 'Your uncle, Mr Brooke, wants me to go on living at the Grange and to help him with his newspaper. I want to stay in this part of the country. I would not feel at home anywhere else.'

'Then I want you to stay too,' Dorothea said. 'I want you to stay very much.'

Will smiled and walked over to the window. But the next moment, Dorothea thought of her husband and his feelings towards his young cousin.

'But that is just my view. You must be guided by Mr Casaubon's wishes, not mine,' she said. 'Why not wait here and ask him about it when he comes home?'

'Not today,' Will said quickly. 'Look, the rain has stopped. I'd better go now, as I am walking back to the Grange. Goodbye.'

'Goodbye,' Dorothea repeated sadly. 'I wish you could have stayed.'

———

Mr Casaubon returned to Lowick Manor later in the afternoon.

'Have you had a good day, dear?' Dorothea asked.

Mr Casaubon smiled and nodded several times.

'Yes, there was interesting conversation at lunch and my work was praised,' he said cheerfully.

'I am so glad,' Dorothea replied. 'I had an interesting conversation too – with Mr Ladislaw.'

Casaubon sighed and closed his eyes.

The Cousins

'My uncle has bought one of the Middlemarch newspapers,' Dorothea went on. 'And he has asked Mr Ladislaw to stay with him and write articles for the paper. My uncle has become interested in politics,' she added. 'Mr Ladislaw wishes to have a steady job and he would like to stay in this part of the country because no one else cares for him. He wanted to know your opinion.'

Mr Casaubon did not answer, but the next morning, he sent his cousin a letter. The letter began:

> *Dear Mr Ladislaw*
>
> *The work that you intend doing in the neighbourhood does not please me. In the past, I have helped you by giving you money and letting you live the life of a gentleman. You should think about my social position before taking up this most unsuitable work.*
>
> *I have no power to stop you, but I do have the power to end any friendship between us. If you take up this position you will no longer be welcome in my house.*
>
> *Edward Casaubon.*

Dorothea had no idea that her husband had sent this letter. She had been thinking how he could help Will Ladislaw. She knew that Mr Casaubon had a great deal of money, all of which he was leaving to her.

'But I have enough money of my own – more than enough –' Dorothea said to herself. 'It would be better if Edward left some of his money to Will. Will was very poor as a child. It would be wrong to keep all this money, when some of it could help him in his career. I am sure that Edward will agree with me.'

Dorothea had no chance to speak to her husband during the day, but she had a chance later that night. As usual, Mr Casaubon slept badly and, after a few hours, he asked Dorothea to light a candle.

'Do you feel ill, dear?' she asked gently.

The Cousins

'No, but I cannot sleep. Perhaps you would read to me for a little while.'

'May I talk to you instead?' Dorothea asked.

'Of course.'

'I have been thinking about money all day,' Dorothea said. 'I have always had too much. It is so unfair, when others, like your Aunt Julia, had so little. You have been generous to Will, her grandson, already, but I have another plan.'

Dorothea was silent for a few moments, but Casaubon did not answer.

'Leave half of your money to Will,' Dorothea went on. 'It is not right that he is poor when we are so rich.'

'Has Mr Ladislaw asked you to say this?' Casaubon said in a cold, angry voice. 'Has he asked you for money?'

'No!' Dorothea said quickly. 'That is very unkind. Of course Will hasn't asked for money. This is my idea and I think that it is a good one.'

'It certainly is not,' Casaubon replied angrily. 'You are a young woman, Dorothea and you know very little about such things. This is not the first time that you have given me a foolish opinion of this kind. Please do not interfere between me and Mr Ladislaw. You are becoming too friendly with Will and as a result, too critical of me, your husband.'

Dorothea's eyes filled with tears and she was glad that her husband could not see them. She was beginning to feel that she was living in a bad dream. She felt very frightened and very unhappy.

The next day, Will Ladislaw answered his cousin's letter. He rejected all Casaubon's suggestions politely, but firmly.

Casaubon himself, spoke to no one about his feelings. He did not want people to know that his marriage was not perfect. He tried to hide his jealousy of Will, but it grew stronger, day by day.

Casaubon was already making plans to make Will's life unpleasant. And he was determined to keep Will and Dorothea apart, whatever happened.

10
Plans

Mr Brooke's latest interest was in local politics, but he was also thinking of standing for Parliament – a Parliament that would be reformed by the will of the people. Although he was not a young man, he was full of enthusiasm. But Mr Brooke's thoughts and ideas were often confused. What he said and what he did, were two different things.

Mr Brooke's friends began to feel worried. Brooke was a very rich man with a big estate, but he was not a good landlord. He did not look after his tenants well and the local farmers often complained about him.

'Your uncle will make a fool of himself, if he tries to stand for Parliament,' Sir James said to Celia. 'People in Middlemarch are not interested in politics, they are interested in their own lives. They will not listen to Brooke's political ideas for the future, because he does not help them now. The Tipton estate is not well-managed, because Brooke tries to do everything himself. He got rid of his farm-manager, Caleb Garth, to save money. Garth was a good worker and Brooke should take him back.'

'Dorothea used to help uncle too,' Celia replied. 'Now she thinks of nothing but her unpleasant old husband and his boring work.'

'Then tell her that you are not feeling well. Invite her here for a few days, by herself,' Sir James said. 'Explain the problem. Then

Plans

we'll take her to the Grange and she can speak to your uncle about the estate. He will listen to her.'

A few days later, Mr Brooke and Will Ladislaw were working together in the library at the Grange. Ladislaw was bored and while Mr Brooke was talking about reform, the young man was thinking of several other things.

When Mrs Casaubon's name was announced, Will stood up, in a state of great excitement. Dorothea's entrance into the room, was like dawn breaking at the start of a perfect day. Will was full of happiness and his mind and body felt completely alive again.

'Well, my dear, this is a pleasant surprise,' Mr Brooke said as he kissed his niece. 'You have left your husband with his books, I suppose. That is right. A woman's mind cannot stand too much learning.'

'You are right, uncle,' Dorothea replied with a smile. 'I often find myself thinking of other things when I am copying my husband's notes. Planning cottages for the villagers of Tipton was much easier than Greek and Latin.'

Dorothea smiled again. 'We all want to improve the lives of poor people,' she went on. 'Sir James tells me that you have so many plans for the Tipton estate. If you go into Parliament, your main concern will be for the people on your own land. Mr Garth can manage the place again and there will be so many improvements. Oh, how I wish that I could help you with them! But now you have Will, of course. What changes you will be able to make and what good you will do together!'

'Now, my dear, we can't go too fast!' her uncle exclaimed. 'I never said that I would do that. But I never said that I would not do that, you know.'

At that moment, a servant came in with a message. Mr Brooke hurried out and Will and Dorothea were left alone.

'I shall not forget that you came here,' Will said quickly. 'You are a good influence on your uncle. I am trying to be one too. As you know, he has many ideas, but they are not always sensible

Plans

ones. But I have to speak to you about something else,' he went on. 'As I may not have another chance to talk about it.'

Dorothea turned and walked towards the open window.

'Please tell me what it is,' she said quietly.

'I suppose you know that your husband has forbidden[71] me to go to his house,' Will began.

'No, I did not,' Dorothea replied. 'I am very, very sorry. I wish I could do something about it. But my husband is very stubborn[72]. He rarely changes his mind about anything. I wonder why he said that to you.'

'He dislikes what I am doing for your uncle,' Will said. 'Mr Casaubon says that it is unsuitable work for a member of his family. I think that is unfair. I am an honourable[73] man and I shall do the work in an honourable way.'

'I am sure you will,' Dorothea said sadly. 'Perhaps we had better not say any more. You will be staying here, I suppose?'

'Yes. But we shall hardly ever see each other.'

'Hardly ever,' Dorothea repeated softly. 'But I shall hear about you. I shall know what you are doing for my uncle.'

'But no one will tell me anything about you,' Will said.

'There will be nothing to tell. I am always at Lowick,' Dorothea replied.

'Lowick Manor is your prison,' Will said quickly.

'Please do not say that. I shall be trying to help others and so will you. I try not to think of my own desires now. My life is easy. The days will pass at Lowick, as they would pass anywhere. And the days will pass for you too.'

'I told you once that I am a rebel,' Will replied with a smile. 'I don't always do what I am told.'

'But if you do what is good, that doesn't matter,' Dorothea said. Then she added, 'I must go now. Celia is expecting me.' And with one last smile, she left Will alone with his thoughts.

When Dorothea returned home to Lowick Manor, she did not tell her husband that she had seen Will Ladislaw. Mr Casaubon

Plans

did not question his wife about her visit. Instead he told her that Doctor Lydgate was coming to see him later that afternoon.

'Have you been feeling unwell, dearest?' Dorothea said quickly. 'I should not have left you alone.'

'No, no. I just want to ask Lydgate a few questions,' Casaubon replied. 'When he calls, I shall be taking my usual walk in the garden nearest to the house. Ask him to meet me there.'

The truth was that Mr Casaubon was deeply unhappy. To his surprise, his marriage to Dorothea had not made his life easier. His wife was good and beautiful, but Mr Casaubon had been troubled to find that she had ideas of her own. She made judgments, and sometimes she criticised his work. She had even suggested that it might never be finished. This thought had upset Mr Casaubon very much and it made him afraid.

Other things were upsetting him too. Will Ladislaw was living nearby and Casaubon hated him. He hated Will's youth, his good-looks and his independence. And most of all, Mr Casaubon feared Will's plans for the future.

Casaubon said to himself, 'I know why he has become so friendly with Brooke. Ladislaw is waiting for me to die. Then he will persuade Dorothea to marry him. Dead or alive, I shall stop that marriage. He will never take what is mine! I must make it impossible for Dorothea ever to think of marrying him.'

So Casaubon had made his plans and then he invited Doctor Lydgate to Lowick Manor.

Lydgate, who was now married to Rosamond Vincy, had just returned from his honeymoon. When he arrived at Lowick he saw Casaubon walking slowly up and down in the garden.

'Poor Casaubon, he is half-dead already,' Lydgate said to himself. 'He is only middle-aged, but he already walks and looks like an old man.'

'Thank you for coming here,' Casaubon said to Lydgate when he saw the young man. 'I have a few questions to ask you. I think that you will give me honest answers.'

Plans

'I will try,' Lydgate replied. 'I have already examined you very carefully, but no doctor can be right all the time. Have you been feeling ill recently?'

'No, not exactly,' Casaubon replied. 'As you know, my life's work is still unfinished. If I die, I want it to be completed by... others. Tell me the truth, Doctor Lydgate. You have examined me. You know all my symptoms[74]. Is my disease fatal? How long do I have to live?'

'Your heart is weak and death could be very sudden. On the other hand, you may live for many years yet,' Lydgate replied. 'No doctor can say for certain.'

'Have you told Mrs Casaubon this?'

'I did suggest it,' Lydgate replied. 'Your wife is a brave woman, Mr Casaubon. She wanted to know the truth.'

Casaubon nodded. 'Thank you. That is all I wanted to know,' he said.

Dorothea saw Doctor Lydgate ride away and she began to walk slowly towards her husband. She smiled at him, but his look was so cold that she felt afraid. When she reached him, she tried to put her arm through his, but he went on alone. He did not want her pity.

They walked slowly into the house and then Mr Casaubon went into the library and shut the door behind him.

Dorothea slowly climbed the stairs up to her own room. It was a beautiful evening, but the poor girl was too unhappy to look out of the window. And she was too angry to cry.

'Why does he treat me like this?' she said to herself. 'Nothing I do is right. He wishes that he had never married me and he will not allow me to help him at all. What do I have to live for?'

That evening, Dorothea's maid, Tantripp, knocked at her door.

'Mr Casaubon is having his dinner in the library. He is very busy, madam,' the maid said quietly. 'Let me bring you something to eat here.'

'No, thank you, Tantripp. I am not well. I shall go to bed soon,' Dorothea replied with a sigh.

She sat alone in the darkness for nearly three hours. Then she stood up and walked to the top of the stairs. The library door opened and her husband began to walk slowly up the stairs towards her. He looked very old and ill.

'Were you waiting for me, Dorothea?' he asked in surprise.

'Yes, I did not like to disturb you,' she replied. For the first time that day, Dorothea felt sorry for her husband. She put her hand in his and they walked along the corridor together.

11

The Answer

Dorothea wanted to know if her husband's illness was getting worse. She did not want to ask Casaubon himself about it, so she decided to visit Lydgate at his home.

Dorothea did not often leave home without her husband, but two days later, she ordered the carriage and was driven into Middlemarch. It was about four o'clock in the afternoon, when the carriage stopped outside the Lydgates' house, but Dorothea was told that Doctor Lydgate was out. Then she remembered that the doctor had recently been married.

'Is Mrs Lydgate at home?' she asked the servant.

'Yes, madam.'

'Then will you ask her if she can see Mrs Casaubon for a few minutes?' Dorothea said.

As she spoke, she heard a man's voice and the sound of a piano coming from the sitting-room of the beautifully-furnished house. Then the maid showed Dorothea into the elegant room and Rosamond walked forward.

The Answer

With a smile, Dorothea held out her hand to Doctor Lydgate's lovely wife.

The two women, who were so very different, had never met before. Rich and important local families like the Chettams and Brookes, did not often meet the trades-people of Middlemarch. They did not belong to the same level of society. The two beautiful young women were dressed very differently too.

Dorothea, as usual, was wearing a very plain, cream-coloured dress and she wore no jewellery except her gold wedding-ring. In contrast, Rosamond was dressed in the latest and most expensive fashion. She wore a pale-blue dress with a large collar. Her small, white hands were covered with rings.

'Thank you for seeing me,' Dorothea said. 'I am anxious to see Dr Lydgate. Could you tell me where I can find him?'

'He is at the New Hospital,' Rosamond replied. 'I can send someone for him at once.'

'Let me go,' Will Ladislaw said, stepping forward.

'Oh, I did not think that I would see you here,' Dorothea said in surprise. Her voice was filled with pleasure at seeing him.

Will moved towards the door, but then Dorothea added,

'Don't worry, Mr Ladislaw. I will drive to the hospital myself. I want to get home as quickly as possible.'

As Will helped Dorothea to her carriage, Dorothea suddenly felt confused. She had been surprised to see him alone with Rosamond Lydgate and she did not know what to think.

Will also felt confused and sad as he watched Dorothea's carriage drive away. He was now living in Middlemarch and he saw a good deal of the Lydgates. But he was able to see Dorothea less and less. He felt that Dorothea had not been pleased to see him at the Lydgates' house. Had Casaubon been turning her against him? Curse[75] him, if he had!

When Will returned to Rosamond, he told her that he had to leave. Rosamond smiled.

'Mrs Casaubon looks very clever. Is she?' Rosamond asked.

The Answer

'You know her quite well, I think.'

'Clever? I have never thought about it,' Will replied crossly.

'You men are so strange!' Rosamond said with a laugh. 'That is exactly what Tertius said when I asked him if Mrs Casaubon was beautiful. What are you both thinking of when you meet her?'

'She is perfect,' Will said. 'That is what I think.'

'Then perhaps I should be jealous when Tertius goes to Lowick,' Rosamond said with a laugh, as Will was leaving. He did not reply.

When her husband was at home again, Rosamond said,

'Mr Ladislaw was here singing with me when Mrs Casaubon came in. Will seemed upset that she had seen him here. Do you know, I think he is deeply in love with Mrs Casaubon. I think that he adores[76] her!'

'Poor fellow,' Lydgate said with a smile.

'Why do you say that?' Rosamond asked.

'Why, when a man adores one of you beauties, he stops thinking about his work and thinks only of her!'

'Well, I am sure you put your work first. You are always at the New Hospital, or seeing poor patients. And when you are here, you are reading a medical book, or looking through your microscope[77] at something unpleasant.'

'I have ambitions, Rosy,' Lydgate replied. 'Wouldn't you like to see me as something more than a Middlemarch doctor? And to be that, I must work and write.'

'I have never stopped you working, Tertius,' Rosamond said, 'but we should go out more. You are not getting tired of me, are you?'

'I love you more than ever, Rosy,' Lydgate said, as he kissed his wife's beautiful face.

'But what did Mrs Casaubon want to see you about today?' Rosamond asked.

'She was worried about her husband's health,' Lydgate replied.

The Answer

'But she is interested in the New Hospital too. I think she will give us two hundred pounds a year! Think what a help that will be!'

Rosamond was quiet for a moment. Then she said, 'I sometimes wish that you were not a doctor, Tertius. You are always talking about money. Medicine is not a nice profession.'

'Please do not say that!' Lydgate cried. 'It upsets me. It is like saying you wish you had married another man. Medicine is the greatest profession in the world, Rosy.'

Will Ladislaw continued to visit the Lydgates. The two men got on well together, although they were so different. Will enjoyed singing with Rosamond too, but his thoughts were always with Dorothea Casaubon.

'Now that I am living in Middlemarch and not at Tipton Manor, I may never see her again,' Will said to himself. And then he remembered that the next day was Sunday.

'If I go to Lowick church tomorrow morning, I shall see her there,' Ladislaw thought. 'Mr Casaubon can't stop me going to church, can he? I may even have a chance to speak to Dorothea herself.'

On Sunday the weather was perfect and Will enjoyed his walk through the fields. He arrived at the church early but the Casaubons were not there. Then at last, Dorothea arrived, followed by her husband, who was not preaching that day.

Dorothea bowed as she passed Will and her face was very pale. Will suddenly felt very uncomfortable and he wished that he had stayed at home. He dared not look at Dorothea and, at the end of the service, the Casaubons left the church first. Again, Dorothea bowed, but this time, her eyes were full of tears. Her husband did not look at Will at all.

Will walked out after them, but they did not stop. In a few minutes, the Casaubons had crossed the churchyard and were in the gardens of Lowick Manor, where Will could not follow them.

The Answer

He walked home sadly, all hope gone.

Dorothea too was very upset as she walked home. It was clear that Mr Casaubon would not change his mind. He was determined never to speak to his young cousin again.

Mr Casaubon was not very well that day and he said very little at lunch. As usual, he spent the afternoon in the library and Dorothea went to her own room. She tried to read, but nothing interested her. More than ever, she wanted something to do, something to make her life worth living.

It was Sunday, so she could not have the carriage to visit Celia, who had recently had a baby. The afternoon passed very slowly for Dorothea. She did not want to read. She did not want to think. It was true. Lowick Manor *was* her prison.

After dinner, Mr Casaubon was more cheerful. He asked Dorothea to follow him into the library, where he had arranged some of his important notebooks on the table. He took up the one containing the main points of his work.

'Please read this aloud to me,' he said. 'When I say "mark" make a mark with your pencil and then read on. This will help you to select the most important ideas and take an intelligent interest in my work.'

They worked for two hours and Dorothea realised that her husband was involving her more closely in his work after his meeting with Lydgate.

At her husband's request, Dorothea took the book up to their bedroom. Mr Casaubon woke up after a few hours, as he usually did and he asked Dorothea to continue reading to him.

'My mind is very clear tonight,' Mr Casaubon said. 'We must work together while we can.'

After nearly two hours, Casaubon said,

'Close the book now, my dear. We will continue working tomorrow. I will sleep now. But, before I do, I have a request to make.'

The Answer

Dorothea suddenly felt afraid.

'What is it?' she said.

'If I die, I shall want you to carry out my wishes,' her husband explained. 'I would want you to follow them exactly. I would need a firm promise from you.'

There was silence.

'Do you refuse this request?' Casaubon asked coldly.

'No, I have not refused yet,' Dorothea replied. 'But I don't know what your wishes are. If I don't know what you want me to do, how can I make a promise?'

'If you refuse, you will be following your own judgment, not mine. You will be refusing to obey me, your husband!'

'No, that is not true,' poor Dorothea answered, almost in tears. 'I want to help you, you know I do. But I must know what I am promising. Give me time to think, dear. I will give you my answer tomorrow.'

'Tomorrow then,' Mr Casaubon agreed coldly.

He soon fell asleep, but there was no more sleep for Dorothea. It was clear to her that if she agreed, the rest of her life would be spent in arranging and re-arranging her husband's notes, whether her husband was alive or dead.

Dorothea at last fell asleep and she woke late. Her maid told her that Mr Casaubon was already in the library and waiting for her.

'You look very pale, madam. I have never seen you so pale,' Tantripp said to her mistress, as she helped her dress. 'Don't go into that dark old library, madam. Sit in the garden and rest. It's a lovely day.'

'Oh, no, Mr Casaubon wants me in the library and I must go,' Dorothea said quickly and she hurried downstairs.

'Where have you been, Dorothea? I have been waiting for you for some time,' Casaubon said. 'I had hoped to start work at once, but I am feeling rather unwell. I shall go and walk in the garden

The Answer

before we begin. Can you give me the answer I want now?'

'Perhaps I could join you there very soon.' Dorothea said quietly. 'I will let you know my answer then.'

Casaubon sighed and nodded.

'You know my favourite walk,' he said. 'I shall be in the garden for the next half-hour. Don't be long, Dorothea. Remember, I am waiting for your answer.'

Casaubon stood up, walked slowly across the room and out into the garden.

Dorothea stayed in the library and she sat there very still. Then, after a time, she rang for Tantripp and asked for her bonnet[78] and shawl[79].

Tantripp had known Dorothea all her life and she knew that something was wrong.

'God bless you, madam,' the maid said. As she put the shawl around the beautiful girl's shoulders, Dorothea began to cry and cry. At last she made herself stand up and walk through the open glass door into the garden.

The poor girl walked very slowly. She felt trapped by her husband's request. All her heart and mind told her to say no, but she knew that she was too weak to refuse him.

She found Casaubon in the summer house[80]. He was sitting very still. His arms were resting on the table in front of him and his hands were covering his face.

'I am here, Edward,' Dorothea said quietly. 'I am ready.'

Casaubon did not answer and Dorothea thought that he was asleep.

'Wake up, dear. Please listen to me,' she said. 'I am ready now, Edward. I am ready to give you my answer.'

But Edward Casaubon was dead. He had not lived long enough to hear the answer that he wanted from his wife.

Later that day, Lydgate was called to Lowick Manor and he sat beside Dorothea's bed as she called her husband's name, over and over again. The poor girl was half-mad with grief.

'Tell Edward I shall go to him soon,' Dorothea cried out. 'Tell him that I am ready to promise. But thinking about it has made me ill, so very ill. I shall soon be better. Go and tell him. Please tell Edward that!'

But it was too late. Now the promise would never be made.

12

Power Beyond the Grave

It was the day after Casaubon's funeral and Dorothea was still too ill to leave her room. Sir James Chettam was in the library at Lowick Manor, talking to Mr Brooke.

'I wish that we could keep the truth about the will from Dorothea,' Sir James was saying angrily. 'She is not well and she should not be upset. She was only married for eighteen months and now this has happened!'

'We can't stop her finding out, Chettam,' Mr Brooke replied. 'Dorothea is an executor[81] of her husband's will and she was twenty-one last December. She will want to know everything. There is nothing we can do about it.'

Sir James thought for a minute and then he said,

'Dorothea must come to live at Freshitt Hall for a time. Being with Celia and the baby will be good for her. Until Dorothea is better, we will deal with any business, not her. And you must get rid of young Ladislaw. Send him out of the country!'

Mr Brooke walked to the window. Then he turned and said,

'I can't do that, Chettam. Ladislaw has been very useful to me. Very useful, you know.'

'But things are different now,' Sir James replied quickly. 'I am Dorothea's brother-in-law and I feel that Casaubon has insulted[82] her. Casaubon was jealous of Ladislaw, we all know that. But why did he have to add those instructions to his will? Now everyone will be gossiping about that young man and your niece. Send him away, Brooke. Send him away!'

'If we send Ladislaw away, people will think that we do not trust Dorothea,' Mr Brooke said. 'But take her to Freshitt with you. That will be the very best thing for her.'

So Dorothea went to Freshitt Hall to stay with Sir James and Celia who did her best to bring a smile to her sister's sad face. Every morning they sat together in a pretty little sitting-room and watched Celia's baby, little Arthur. But even her wonderful little nephew could not make Dorothea smile.

Brooke was right when he had predicted that Dorothea would want to know everything. It was less than a week before she began to think about her husband's will.

'Perhaps Sir James would drive me over to Lowick,' Dorothea said to her sister. 'I want to look at all my husband's papers. I must see his will too, of course. Edward may have left some instructions for me,' she added, and her eyes were full of tears.

'You are not to go until Doctor Lydgate says you can go,' Celia said. 'You'll upset yourself. You think there is something unpleasant in the will, don't you, my dear?'

'What are you talking about, Celia?' Dorothea asked. 'Now *you're* upsetting me. What unpleasant thing? I don't know what you mean.'

'Then I'd better tell you,' Celia answered calmly. 'He – your husband – Mr Casaubon, added some new instructions to his will. Everything – land, property, money, everything – will be taken away from you if you marry…'

'Marry? I'll never marry!' Dorothea said quickly.

'…if you marry Mr Ladislaw,' Celia went on. 'Not anyone else. Just Mr Ladislaw.'

Dorothea blushed and her eyes filled with tears. She did not know what to say or do. Her dead husband had insulted her from beyond the grave and she hated him for it.

Dorothea had never before thought of Will Ladislaw as a lover, but now the idea took hold of her mind for the first time. Had Will ever thought of her in that way? She would never know. How could they ever see each other again?

They could never be friends now.

At that moment Dr Lydgate was announced. He entered the room to see Dorothea looking very pale in her black widow's[83] clothes.

'You are not well, Mrs Casaubon,' he said kindly.

'I agree,' Celia said. 'She wants to go over to Lowick to look at some papers. I think she should stay here and rest.'

Lydgate thought for a moment before replying. Then he said, 'Mrs Casaubon should be allowed to do what she wants.'

So Dorothea was driven back to Lowick Manor for a short time. She looked everywhere, but found nothing new. Casaubon had wanted his wife to spend the rest of her life completing his work. He had made that clear to her. But he had died before Dorothea had given him her answer.

Edward Casaubon no longer had any power over Dorothea's life and now she had no pity for him at all. Casaubon's last wish had shown his true feelings and Dorothea hated the idea of his money.

Dorothea returned to Freshitt and she stayed there until the end of June.

Will Ladislaw was busy helping Mr Brooke with his political work. The young man was working hard and heard nothing of the gossip about Mr Casaubon and his will. But Ladislaw noticed that Mr Brooke did not invite him to Tipton Grange so often.

'I am being kept away from Mrs Casaubon,' Will said to himself. 'We are divided forever and in so many different ways. She has property and a high place in local society. I am a poor stranger and half-foreign too. We could not be more different.

While Dorothea is staying at Freshitt, I can never see her. Sir James hates my politics, because he hates all change. Mr Brooke wants to be a reformer, but he will never succeed in Middlemarch. He does not look after his estate and people here do not respect him.'

Will was right about the people of Middlemarch. Mr Brooke wished to serve his country by standing for Parliament. He had bought the *Pioneer* newspaper to express his ideas on reforming English politics. But, before he was accepted as a candidate, Mr Brooke had to speak to the people of Middlemarch. In his speech, he had to convince the townspeople that he was the best man to represent them.

The time for Mr Brooke's speech had come. He walked out onto the balcony of the White Hart Inn. He smiled and looked down at all the people who had crowded into the market-place to hear him.

'Gentlemen! Electors[84] of Middlemarch!' Mr Brooke began. 'I am very happy to be here, proud and happy.'

The crowd was silent. Will had written down the main points of Mr Brooke's speech for him, but he was not sure what Mr Brooke would say.

'You know me. I am your neighbour!' Mr Brooke went on. 'I have always tried to help you – you, the good people of Middlemarch. But the world is a big place. The traders and manufacturers of Middlemarch send their goods to many different countries. That is right. Now Middlemarch must follow new ideas – new ideas you know, from other countries. I must play my part and so must you!'

'Must?' someone shouted. 'In Middlemarch we do what's best for ourselves – not for other countries!'

'Or for rich landlords like you!' someone else called out.

Some of the crowd laughed and cheered. Another voice shouted,

He smiled and looked down at all the people who had crowded into the market-place to hear him.

'Curse your ideas. People like you don't know what reform is! We want the Bill! We want real reform. Down with the landlords!'

The crowd cheered again, more loudly than before.

'We all want reform – liberty, freedom and so on,' Mr Brooke went on.

'Then start with your own estate,' another man shouted. 'There's not much freedom there! Repair the farm buildings. Pay your men better wages! Bring back Garth to put things in order! Then we may listen to you and your talk of reform!'

At that moment, someone threw an egg at Mr Brooke. It hit him on the shoulder. Several more eggs followed. Men in the crowd began to shout and laugh.

Mr Brooke went on speaking for a little longer, but no one could hear him. In the end, he left the balcony, shaking his head sadly.

'They did not listen. They did not give me time,' Mr Brooke said to Will. 'They are not ready, not ready for reform, you know,' he added.

'They are not ready for anything new,' Will replied. He was angry with Mr Brooke and angry with himself too. He needed to think about what to do next.

'People are laughing at Brooke now and they will soon be laughing at me,' Will told himself when he was alone. 'Dorothea will not thank me for helping her uncle make a fool of himself and her friends will blame me too. I must get away – yes, I'll go to London and study law. In five years' time I could be a successful politician – even famous, perhaps. Then I can return to Middlemarch as Dorothea's equal and tell her how I feel. But how do I know that she will wait for me? I'll have to stay a little longer. I must know how she feels before I go.'

The next day, Mr Brooke asked Will to Tipton Grange.

'I think that I must give up the *Pioneer*,' Brooke told him. 'I am not a young man, Ladislaw. You may stand for Parliament one day, but I never will now. You have a bright future in front of you, I'm sure, but not, perhaps, in Middlemarch.'

'I am very grateful to you,' Will said proudly. 'But you should not worry about what I decide to do next.'

'I am going away for a time,' Mr Brooke went on. 'Middlemarch is a small place, you know. A young man like you would do better in London.'

Will thought that he understood Mr Brooke very well.

'The family would like to get rid of me,' Will said to himself. 'But I shall go when I want to go and not before. And I must see Dorothea first.'

Some time later, Dorothea decided to return to Lowick Manor. The library was opened again and light filled that dark room once more. The young widow walked through all the rooms of the sad house, thinking about the eighteen months of her married life.

Then she went back to the library and arranged all her husband's notebooks carefully. Was one of them missing?

Dorothea looked through all the drawers in her husband's desk again. At the back of one of them, she saw an envelope that she had not seen before. In the envelope was the missing note-book. She opened it.

> *Table of Contents. Listing the main points of my life's work.*
>
> *For the use of Mrs Casaubon, who will complete it after my death.*

Dorothea shook her head and smiled sadly. Then she put the note-book back and wrote on the envelope:

> *I could not do it. Surely you can see that? I could not work for the rest of my life at something I do not believe in.*

Dorothea put the envelope in her own desk and never opened it again.

Then she stood up, sighed, and looked out into the garden. It was full of light and colour but it did not please her, because her heart was sad. She longed[85] to see Will Ladislaw, but she was not even sure that he was in Middlemarch.

'There is no one I can ask,' Dorothea thought to herself. 'Perhaps Will has heard about my husband's wishes. Perhaps he does not want to see me again. But, oh, how I long to see him!'

One morning, a few days later, Dorothea was sitting in her own room. She was trying to work out her income[86], but instead, she was looking out of the window, at the scene she knew so well. Everything was still and quiet. Nothing moved.

'It is like my life,' Dorothea said to herself. 'It will never change now. Things will go on from day to day and I shall be here for the rest of my life.'

At that moment, Tantripp came in and said,

'Mr Ladislaw is downstairs, madam. He would like to see you, if it is not too early.'

'Show Mr Ladislaw into the sitting-room. I shall see him there,' Dorothea said quickly.

This meeting was very different from their first meeting in Rome. Then Will had been embarrassed and Dorothea had been calm. Now Dorothea's heart was beating very fast as she came into the room. Will turned to look at her. She was dressed completely in black and her face was pale. But she looked very beautiful, perhaps more beautiful than she had ever been before. They walked towards each other and Dorothea held out her hand.

'Let us sit near the window. It is such a lovely day,' Dorothea said quietly.

'I hope that you do not mind my calling,' Will said quickly. 'I did not wish to leave the neighbourhood and begin a new life without saying goodbye to you.'

'It would have been unkind of you to leave without seeing me,' Dorothea replied with a smile. 'Are you going away at once?'

'Very soon,' Will replied. 'I am going to London, where I hope to train as a barrister[87].

'Working with your uncle has made me more interested in politics,' Will went on. 'Things are changing in England. I would like to be part of those changes. Other men without family or money have led successful and useful lives. I want to do the same.'

'And I am sure that you will,' Dorothea said with a sweet smile. 'You care for honour and justice. You care for people.'

'So you approve of my going away, perhaps for years?' Will said. He wanted so much to know what Dorothea was thinking, but she did not answer at once.

Dorothea turned and stared out of the window. It was a long time before she spoke.

'I will be happy when I hear you have done well,' she said at last. 'But we will have to be patient. It may be a... a... long... while.'

When Dorothea said that, so slowly and sadly, Will wanted to take her in his arms, but he dared not.

'You will forget all about me,' he said.

'No,' Dorothea said. 'I shall never forget you. I do not know many people and very little happens at Lowick. I shall have plenty of time to think about you.'

At hearing this, Will stood up suddenly and walked across to a table. He leant against it, hat in hand. Blood had rushed into his cheeks. He wanted Dorothea to know his true feelings, but he did not dare tell her. He had no idea what the beautiful young widow thought about him.

'May I give you this portrait of your grandmother?' Dorothea said, holding out the little painting. 'She looks so very like you.'

'No, no,' Will replied quickly. 'I would be happier if someone else wanted it for that reason. I have very few things of my own. Why would I want that?'

'You are happier than me,' Dorothea said sadly. 'You have nothing, but I have too much.'

Will looked surprised. 'How can poverty be good when it keeps me from what I most care for?' he asked.

'Sometimes silence does the same,' Dorothea said sadly. 'When we cannot find words…'

At that moment, her butler, Pratt, came into the room and said,

'Sir James Chettam is in the library, madam.'

'Ask him to come in here,' Dorothea replied, without thinking.

Will and Dorothea stood in silence until Sir James came into the room. He shook hands with Dorothea and bowed coldly to Will Ladislaw. Sir James did not approve of Will and he was unhappy to see him alone with Dorothea. Will understood this and he decided to leave at once.

'I must say goodbye, Mrs Casaubon,' he said. 'It will be goodbye for a long time.'

Will's pride would not let him say more. With one last look, he shook hands with Dorothea, bowed to Sir James and left the room.

Sir James did not realize how much he had hurt Will's pride by his coldness. By coming into the room at that moment, Sir James had made it impossible for Will and Dorothea to explain their feelings for each other before Will left Middlemarch. If Sir James had known that, he would have been very satisfied. But he did not understand that any hope of future happiness had gone from Dorothea's heart. When she looked at the little portrait of Will's grandmother again, she cried, because it reminded her of Will.

'I wonder when he will be leaving Middlemarch,' Dorothea asked herself. 'He will never come here again. It might be years, before we meet again. I must make a new life for myself,' she thought. 'I own a lot of land now and I cannot look after it all myself. Caleb Garth is working for my uncle again and he can work for me too. There are poor people in the villages that I can help. Thinking about their problems will help me forget mine.'

Will stayed on in Middlemarch for some time, but Dorothea did not know it. No one in her family talked about him and she dared not ask whether he had left the town or not.

13
Marriage Problems

Doctor Lydgate was finding marriage very expensive. Rosamond Lydgate had been spoilt all her life and she expected her husband to spoil her too. She always bought the very best of everything and now they were spending far too much money. Lydgate warned his wife that they were getting into debt[88], but Rosamond refused to listen.

Then Rosamond found that she was expecting a baby. They were both delighted and Rosamond was soon making baby-clothes. One of Lydgate's rich relations, young Captain Lydgate, was staying with them at the time. Rosamond was pleased, because he was happy to flirt[89] with her and Rosamond was happy to let him. But her husband disliked the young man and thought he was a fool.

'You enjoy talking to Will Ladislaw,' Rosamond said. 'Why don't you talk to the Captain at dinner? He is your cousin, after all.'

'Will is an intelligent man,' Lydgate replied. 'Captain Lydgate is not.'

Then, one afternoon, the Captain took Rosamond out riding. She rode well and she enjoyed herself very much. But when her husband heard about it, he was angry.

Marriage Problems

'It is not safe for you to ride at the moment, Rosy,' he said. 'If there is an accident, you could lose the baby.'

Rosamond smiled and shook her pretty head. 'The Captain's horses are very quiet. Nothing will happen, Tertius,' she said.

'How do you know?' Lydgate asked. 'You were safe this time, but you must not go riding again. There is always a chance of an accident.'

'There is chance of an accident if I stay indoors,' Rosamond laughed.

'Don't be silly dear,' Lydgate replied. 'I am your doctor, as well as your husband. I say you must not ride again. It is too dangerous. I shall talk to the Captain myself.'

'Please do not treat me like a child, Tertius,' Rosamond said. 'Don't say anything to the Captain. Leave it to me.'

'Very well,' Lydgate said.

But Rosamond did not mean to obey her husband – and she had promised nothing.

The next time Lydgate was out, Rosamond went riding again with the Captain. At first, her horse was very quiet, but then a sudden noise frightened it into a gallop and for a short while Rosamond lost control. Rosamond was badly shaken. In a few days, she lost the baby, but she refused to believe that the ride was the cause. Lydgate was very angry and his cousin left Middlemarch soon afterwards.

Lydgate was spending more and more time at the New Hospital. He was not given any money for his work there and it stopped him finding more patients. Most of his patients were poor and he was not making as much money as he had hoped.

Before his marriage, Lydgate had never had much money, but he had had enough. Now he was in debt. The rent on the house was high and he had spent more money than he wanted to on furnishing it. Rosamond was fond of entertaining[90] and she always bought the very best of everything for her guests. Rosamond herself was always beautifully dressed and she loved jewellery too.

Marriage Problems

Lydgate was beginning to realize that they could not pay their bills. He knew that he would have to get some money from somewhere, but he refused to ask the Vincys for anything and he tried to think of another way. At first, he said nothing to Rosamond, but when she was well again, he decided that he must talk to her. Lydgate himself was very unhappy. He knew that Rosamond would not understand the problem.

It was evening when Lydgate got home. He had been working hard all day and he was very tired. As he walked into the house, he heard the piano and the sound of singing.

'Ladislaw is here, then,' Lydgate said to himself. 'I don't mind him coming – he keeps Rosy happy. But I must speak to her alone.'

Lydgate walked into the room and sat down. His face was pale and he did not smile at his wife as he usually did. Rosamond saw at once that her husband was in a bad mood.

'How are you, Lydgate?' Will said cheerfully. Lydgate nodded, but he did not reply.

'You are very late, Tertius,' Rosamond said. 'Have you dined?'

'I have. But I would like some tea,' Lydgate said, in an angry voice.

Will could see that Lydgate was upset.

'It is time for me to go,' he said, picking up his hat.

'Please stay,' Rosamond said with a smile. 'Tertius is in a bad mood about something and he won't speak to me all evening!'

'Yes, I will. I have something very important to discuss with you,' Lydgate said to his wife.

'Then I must go. Goodbye,' Will said quickly, and he left the room.

A servant brought in the tea-things and put them on a table. Rosamond sat down and began to pour out the tea. Lydgate looked at her sadly. He was remembering Dorothea's words, that she had lived only to help her husband.

'Would Rosy say the same about me? I don't think so,' the young doctor thought sadly.

Marriage Problems

'Here is your tea, Tertius,' Rosamond said. Then she walked back across the room, without looking at him.

They sat in silence until the servant had taken away the tea-things and brought in the candles.

'Dear Rosy, come here and sit near me,' Lydgate said quietly.

Rosamond obeyed. To her husband, she was as beautiful as ever. He held her hand in his and said,

'I have to tell you something that will upset you, Rosy. But we are husband and wife and we must share everything, good or bad. I expect you have realized that I am short of money.'

Rosamond said nothing, but she turned her head away and looked at a picture at the other end of the room.

'I spent a lot of money before we were married and I have been spending money ever since,' Lydgate went on. 'We owe the furniture warehouse three hundred and eighty pounds. We must think about this problem together, Rosy, and you must help me.'

'What can *I* do, Tertius?' Rosamond asked in surprise.

Lydgate sighed. He knew that Rosamond would not understand.

'The manufacturer wants security for our debt,' Lydgate said. 'The men are coming tomorrow to make an inventory[91] – to work out the price of everything we have.'

'Haven't you asked Papa for the money?' Rosamond asked.

'No.'

'Then I will ask him,' Rosamond said, standing up and walking away from her husband.

'No, Rosy. It is too late to do that. The men are coming tomorrow. They will make a list, as I told you. Nothing else will happen. We will find the money to pay for everything somehow. But I don't want your father to know about it.'

Then Rosamond's beautiful eyes filled with tears and she began to cry.

Marriage Problems

'Please, Rosy dear. It is all my fault, I know. We have spent too much money. You must help me to be more careful. If we can try to save a little, we will soon be out of debt.'

'Send the men away when they come tomorrow,' Rosamond said calmly. 'They can come back some other time.'

'You are not listening to me, Rosy,' Lydgate replied angrily. 'I shall not send them away. I cannot.'

'Then we must leave Middlemarch. There will be a sale and everything will be sold. We can go to live in London.'

'We can't go anywhere without money, Rosamond,' Lydgate said.

'Then someone must help us,' she replied.

'No. We must help ourselves. Look at this list,' Lydgate went on. 'This other place will take back some of the cutlery[92].'

'So we shall have to eat without knives or forks!' Rosamond cried.

'No, of course not, dear,' Lydgate said. 'We have bought too much of everything, that is all. They would take back some of your jewellery too, but I am not asking you to return that.'

Rosamond walked out of the room and returned a few minutes later. She was carrying some small leather boxes, which she put down on a table.

'This is all the jewellery you ever gave me,' she said coldly. 'Return what you like and the cutlery too. But do not expect me to be here tomorrow. I shall go to Papa's.'

'It would be better if you stayed,' Lydgate said. 'It is not right to leave it to the servants. But keep your jewels. Let's try to make the best of things, darling. Kiss me, Rosy.'

The next day, Rosamond asked her father for some money, but he only replied,

'Trade is bad at the moment. I shall soon be needing to borrow money myself. I can't help you.'

14

The Last Goodbye?

Fred Vincy did not see much of his sister, Rosamond, now that she was married. Fred was working hard too. He had gone back to Oxford and this time, he had taken his degree. But Fred had decided to take Mary Garth's advice. He had not become a clergyman. Instead, he had taken up farming and was now helping Caleb Garth, Mary's father. In time, Fred wanted to be a farm-manager like Mr Garth and then, perhaps, he could have his own farm, where he could try out his own ideas.

Rosamond did not like the idea of Fred being a farmer. She did not consider that farming was a suitable occupation for a Vincy, especially one who had a degree from Oxford.

One afternoon, Fred called at the Lydgates' house, with a message from his mother, Mrs Vincy. Will Ladislaw was leaving as Fred arrived and the young man remembered a story he had heard.

Fred knew little about Ladislaw and the Casaubons. But he had heard about Mr Casaubon's will and, as they had nothing else to talk about, Fred passed the story on to his sister.

'Old Casaubon was jealous of his cousin,' Fred said. 'Before he died, he added some instructions to his will. What do you think they were, Rosy?'

Rosamond was interested in anything to do with Will Ladislaw.

'I've no idea,' Rosamond replied. 'Tell me, Fred, quickly.'

'Well Casaubon left all his money to Mrs Casaubon, of course. But if she marries Will Ladislaw, she'll get nothing!' Fred said with a laugh.

Rosamond was very surprised and she repeated what Fred had told her to her husband that same evening.

The Last Goodbye?

'I have something very interesting to tell you, Tertius,' she said. 'It is about Will and Mrs Casaubon and it is such a romantic story!'

Lydgate listened to Rosamond in silence. He had already heard the story, but he had thought it was too serious to gossip about. Ladislaw was the doctor's friend and now Lydgate had a great respect for Dorothea too. Lydgate was sure that Will and Dorothea were deeply in love. That would explain why Will had still not left Middlemarch. Lydgate felt sorry for them both.

'Take care that you do not mention this to Ladislaw, Rosy,' Lydgate said. 'It would not be fair. All this gossip would upset him very much.'

Rosamond turned her head and smiled, but she said nothing. She knew that Will admired her beauty and enjoyed her company, but she knew that he admired Dorothea Casaubon too.

'Some people think that Mrs Casaubon is beautiful, although she dresses so plainly,' Rosamond said to herself. 'Can Will Ladislaw really be in love with her?'

Rosamond looked at herself in the mirror and smiled. 'I don't think he is,' she thought. 'Mrs Casaubon never wears any jewellery, she dresses plainly and her hair is arranged in a most old-fashioned way.'

When Will called a few days later, Rosamond was alone.

'So you are still in Middlemarch, Mr Ladislaw!' she said with a sweet smile. 'What is keeping you here when everyone thought you were going to London? Wait! Don't tell me. I am sure that I know the answer.'

'I am sure you do,' Will said with a bow, but he was already feeling angry.

'It is a most romantic story!' Rosamond went on. 'Mr Casaubon had guessed the truth before he died and he made his plans well. He knew that there was only one man that his widow would like to marry. But Mr Casaubon's will says that she will lose all

The Last Goodbye?

her property if she does! Oh, dear, isn't that a romantic story? A jealous old husband and a young lover! And then a beautiful widow! Tell me how it will end, Mr Ladislaw!'

'What are you talking about?' Ladislaw cried. 'Tell me the truth! Tell me what you mean!'

'You don't know?' Rosamond asked in surprise.

'No!'

'So you don't know what Mr Casaubon wrote in his will? If Mrs Casaubon marries you, she will lose everything.'

'How did you hear about this? How do you know that it is true?' Ladislaw asked angrily.

'My brother Fred told me,' Rosamond replied. 'And he heard it from a friend of Mr Brooke's. But I am sure there will be a happy ending. Mrs Casaubon likes you better than the property, I'm sure!'

'Please do not say any more,' Will said. 'The story is an insult to Mrs Casaubon and to myself.'

'Please don't be angry with me,' Rosamond replied. 'You should be glad that I told you.'

'Yes, yes. I am.'

'Then I suppose the marriage will be very soon!' Rosamond said with a laugh.

'Not soon. Not ever,' Will replied, as he bowed to her and walked quickly from the room.

Left alone, Rosamond sighed. She was jealous of Will's feelings for Dorothea.

'My life is so dull. What do I have to live for?' she asked herself sadly.

Will knew what he had to do. He had to speak to Dorothea one more time and then leave Middlemarch for ever.

Will wrote to Dorothea and told her that he had not left Middlemarch, but that he would be doing so very soon. He asked her permission to call at Lowick Manor for the last time.

The Last Goodbye?

Two months had passed since Will's 'last words' to Dorothea. But Casaubon's will had changed things. Will did not know that Dorothea had money of her own. He thought that, if they married, Dorothea would have no money at all. Will could not allow that to happen.

But when Will's letter reached Lowick Manor, Dorothea was not there. Her uncle, Mr Brooke, was coming home from his journey to the north. As soon as Dorothea had heard the news of her uncle's return, she had driven to Freshitt Hall, to tell her sister and Sir James. Sir James knew that Will had not left Middlemarch and he had decided to speak to Dorothea about him. Sir James wanted to be sure that Dorothea would not see that young man again.

'I'm glad that your uncle has given up politics,' Sir James said when he and Dorothea were alone. 'But Ladislaw hasn't given up his friends in Middlemarch. People are beginning to talk about him and Doctor Lydgate's wife. Ladislaw is always at their house, singing or flirting with her. She is very beautiful, you know.'

'I do not like gossip,' Dorothea said angrily. 'I will not listen to stories about Mr Ladislaw. He is an honourable man who has had a difficult life. The people of Middlemarch do not understand him, because he is so different from them.'

Dorothea's face was very red and Sir James could see that her eyes were full of tears.

'I am going to Tipton now,' she said. 'The servants have to get the house ready for my uncle's return.'

Sir James walked back with Dorothea to her carriage and bowed as it drove away.

The countryside looked beautiful, but tears ran down Dorothea's face and she could see nothing.

'The people of Middlemarch are mean and hateful,' she whispered to herself. 'The gossip is not true. It is not true.'

Then Dorothea remembered the time when she had seen Mrs Lydgate and Will together.

The Last Goodbye?

'But they were only singing,' Dorothea said to herself. 'He would never do anything wrong. I believe that he is good and I trust him. I must trust him,' she repeated.

By now, she was outside Tipton Grange. Dorothea wiped away her tears and stepped out of the carriage.

'I shall be here about half-an-hour,' she told the driver. She walked into the house and took off her bonnet and gloves. When she saw the housekeeper, Dorothea said,

'I have some instructions from my uncle, Mrs Kell. I shall go into the library and write them down for you. Please open the shutters[93] in there.'

'The shutters are already open,' Mrs Kell said. 'Mr Ladislaw is in the library, looking for some of his sketches.'

At the sound of Will's name, Dorothea's heart nearly stopped beating. Then she was filled with a feeling of complete happiness. She walked down the corridor and the housekeeper followed.

'Go in first and tell Mr Ladislaw that I am here,' Dorothea said to the servant quietly.

Ladislaw was at the other end of the room looking at some sketches that he had left behind. The housekeeper walked towards him.

'Mrs Casaubon is coming in, sir,' she said.

Will looked up quickly as Dorothea came into the room. The housekeeper went out and shut the door behind her.

Without knowing what she was doing, Dorothea walked towards her uncle's chair. Will moved the chair for her and she sat down, Then he moved away and stood looking at her.

'Please sit down,' Dorothea said. 'I am very glad you are here.'

'I am glad too,' Will replied, as he sat down opposite her. 'I sent you a letter. I could not leave without seeing you again.'

'I thought that we said goodbye many weeks ago,' Dorothea answered quietly. 'You thought that you were leaving Middlemarch then.'

The Last Goodbye?

'Yes. But I have learnt things that have changed my feelings about the future. The last time I saw you, I dreamed of returning some day. Now I know more, I don't think that I will ever come back.'

'Do you wish to tell me why?' Dorothea asked.

'Yes, yes. Of course I do,' Will replied.

He walked towards the window and then went on,

'I have been insulted – you know it and other people know it too. I would never have tried to get your money by saying... by pretending that I... It was unjust of Mr Casaubon, very unjust. He has made me seem mean and dishonourable.'

'Never in my eyes,' Dorothea said. 'I have always believed in your honesty.'

She stood up and moved towards the window, but Will turned away from her.

'I trust you. I always have,' Dorothea said, very quietly.

Will stood up and moved back to the table to pick up his sketches.

'I must go,' he said.

'What will you do with your life?' Dorothea asked. 'Are your plans the same as they were before?'

'Yes,' he replied. 'I shall work hard. But I shall be living without happiness and without hope.'

'Oh, what sad words!' Dorothea cried. 'Surely you are speaking too strongly. We both do that, when we are unhappy, I think.'

'I am not speaking too strongly now,' Will said. 'I have seen the best and I have lost it. That only happens to a man once in his life and it has happened to me too soon. I stood at the gates of heaven, but I could not go in. I have lost all hope of happiness.'

Will looked at Dorothea as he spoke.

'Surely she can't misunderstand me?' he thought. 'She must know that I love her. But we can never marry now. She must know that too.'

The Last Goodbye?

But Dorothea had no real experience of love. She did not look at Will. She was too confused and unhappy to understand him.

'He is telling me that he loves Mrs Lydgate,' Dorothea thought. 'That is why he is leaving Middlemarch.'

Neither of them knew what to say next. Then, at last, Will picked up his sketches.

'I must go,' he said. 'I shall leave Middlemarch the day after tomorrow.'

'That is very honest of you,' Dorothea said.

She held out her hand and Will took it for a moment. They looked at each other in silence and then Dorothea said,

'Please remember me!'

'How can you say that when I am in danger of forgetting everything else!' Will cried angrily, and then he had gone.

At that moment, Dorothea understood the truth for the first time. Will loved her. She was truly loved for the first time in her life. She would never meet Will Ladislaw again, but he loved her.

Dorothea wrote out the instructions for the housekeeper and in a few minutes more she was sitting in her carriage again.

'How I wish that I could have helped him!' Dorothea thought to herself. 'But I know that we can never marry – Edward made that impossible.'

She looked out of the window and saw Will walking along the road. Then the carriage had passed him.

Will watched it grow smaller and smaller.

'How will I ever know if she loved me or not?' he said to himself.

Will spent that evening with the Lydgates. The next morning, he had gone.

15
Money Matters

Mr Joshua Rigg Featherstone had inherited Stone Court from his father, but he did not enjoy living there. He soon decided to sell the house and the land around it and return to London.

Mr Nicholas Bulstrode, the banker, had wanted to buy a house with some land for a long time and this was his chance. He bought Stone Court and paid Caleb Garth to look after the land for him. Mr Bulstrode went on living in his house in Middlemarch, because it was near his bank.

Mr Bulstrode had not been born in Middlemarch, but he had lived in the town for many years. He had become very rich and he was generous with his money. He had started to work with Doctor Lydgate on the plans for the New Hospital in the town and the young man was glad of the banker's help.

The people of Middlemarch respected Mr Bulstrode, but they did not like him. He had married Mr Vincy's sister, many years before, but they knew nothing about his family and his early life. Everyone thought that he was too proud of his position in the town and too fond of telling them what to do. Now, as the owner of Stone Court, Bulstrode was one of the most important people in the neighbourhood. He felt happy and secure.

But Mr Bulstrode had a secret in his past. And, one day, that secret came to Middlemarch.

It was early evening and Mr Bulstrode was standing outside Stone Court when he saw a man whom he recognized, although he had not seen him for many years. The man coming towards him was now about sixty years old. He was fat, with short legs and a round, red face.

Mr Bulstrode's pale face went paler as the man called his name.

Money Matters

'Well Nick,' the man cried. 'This is a fine place, a very fine place. A man could live here and be happy.'

'John Raffles. I thought you were in America,' Nicholas Bulstrode said unhappily. 'Why have you come here?'

'Well, not to see you, or not at first. I thought this place belonged to my step-son, Joshua Rigg, but then I heard in the town that you had bought the house. I came to look at it and here you are!

'You must have made plenty of money, Nick,' the man went on. 'Your first wife was rich, of course. A rich widow called Mrs Dunkirk. And we know how she got her money, don't we?'

Nicholas Bulstrode did not answer and Raffles laughed.

'I'm sure that you have kept it a secret all these years,' he said. 'Middlemarch is a long way from London, after all. It was a family business, wasn't it. Nick? The family called it a pawnbroker's[94] shop, didn't they? But the business was more than that.

'Let me think now,' Raffles went on: 'Buying and selling stolen goods. Lending money at high interest. Stealing from the poor, to make the family rich. Paying the police to keep quiet… Not a pretty business, was it, Nick? And you were in charge of it. Then the owner died and you married his widow. Luckily for you, her only child, a daughter, had run away from home. What was her name, now?'

'Sarah Dunkirk,' Bulstrode said quietly.

'That's the name – Sarah. But she had left, so you got all the Dunkirks' money. That was not fair, Nick, not fair at all.'

'The daughter could not be found,' Bulstrode said quickly.

'That is a lie, Nick,' Raffles replied. 'I found her for you, but you did nothing about it. Sarah was married by then – to a poor man with a foreign name. Polish, I think, but I can't remember it now. All that happened in London, of course, a long time ago. But I'm sure it would interest the good people of Middlemarch!'

'I suppose you want money,' Bulstrode said quietly.

Money Matters

Raffles laughed. 'Everyone wants money,' he said. 'But if you are willing to give me some of yours, Nick, that would please me very much. One hundred pounds now perhaps and more when I want it.'

'I would be willing to pay you money to leave Middlemarch – and to stay away,' Bulstrode replied.

But Raffles shook his head.

'I don't want to make a promise that I could not keep,' he said, with a smile on his round, red face. 'I'll have a drink with you now, Nick and your housekeeper can find me something to eat. I think I'll stay here tonight.'

In the new year, Lydgate realized that his debts were increasing and that he had no way of paying them back. He now owed nearly a thousand pounds and he decided to talk to Rosamond again.

'Our expenses are still too high, Rosy dear,' he said. 'I must manage with one horse and perhaps you can manage the house with one servant, not three.'

'Only one servant? What would people think of us?' Rosamond replied. 'No important people would want you as their doctor. You have too many poor patients and you spend too much time at the New Hospital. My uncle Bulstrode should pay you for the work you do there.'

'That is not possible,' Lydgate said angrily. 'My work is my business, not yours. But there is something that we can do.'

'It is something unpleasant, I suppose,' Rosamond said coldly.

Lydgate sighed. 'I think that we should move into a smaller house,' he said. 'This one is too big for us and the rent is too high. I know someone who is looking for a good house. I'll speak to Mr Trumbull, the agent[95], tomorrow.'

Rosamond stood up and walked away from her husband, trying to hide her tears. Then she spoke very slowly.

'I cannot believe that you would like to do that.'

Money Matters

'*Like!* Of course I don't like it!' Lydgate cried angrily. 'But it's the only thing I can do.'

'We could have a sale and leave Middlemarch for good,' Rosamond said.

'Then I would have to start all over again,' Lydgate replied.

'Well then, that would be your own fault, Tertius,' Rosamond said. 'You should have been more polite to your family. Then you could ask them for help now.'

'Never,' Lydgate replied. 'We must move. There is no other way.'

Rosamond left the room without answering him, but she had made up her mind. *She* would find another way. They would never move into a smaller house.

Rosamond was very calm at breakfast the next morning.

'Have you spoken to the agent about this house yet, Tertius?' she asked.

'No, but I shall call on him this morning,' Lydgate said. He kissed his wife as he left the room, glad that she now agreed with the plan.

Rosamond had always left business matters to her husband, but she realized that now she must speak to Mr Trumbull herself. Later that day, she went to the agent's office.

Mr Trumbull bowed politely and Rosamond sat down.

'Has my husband spoken to you about our house?' she asked with a smile.

'Yes, ma'am, yes he did,' Mr Trumbull replied. 'Doctor Lydgate spoke to me this morning. He said that he wanted everything done as quickly as possible and, of course, I shall do what I can.'

'There has been a mistake. We shall not be moving,' Rosamond said. 'Please do nothing more about it. Forget everything that Doctor Lydgate said. Do you understand?'

'Of course, Mrs Lydgate,' Mr Trumbull replied.

Money Matters

That evening, Lydgate noticed that Rosamond seemed much happier. She did not mention the house at first, but, later on, she said,

'Tell me, Tertius. How much money do you need altogether? So that we can stay in this house, I mean.'

'We cannot stay here. I have already told you that, Rosy,' Lydgate said.

'You must know how much,' she repeated quietly. 'Please Tertius, tell me.'

'To clear all the debts and have a little over to live on – one thousand pounds,' Lydgate said. 'But there is no point in telling you that. I haven't got it and never will have.'

Rosamond did not reply. But the next day, she wrote to her husband's uncle, the baronet, whose name was Sir Godwin Lydgate.

In her letter, Rosamond explained to Sir Godwin that Middlemarch was not a good place for his nephew to live. If they moved to London, Tertius would soon be wealthy and popular. But first, he needed one thousand pounds to clear his debts.

In her own mind, poor, silly Rosamond was sure that Tertius would approve of her letter and so she did not tell him that she had sent it. And she did not tell Sir Godwin that the request for money was her idea and not her husband's.

Time went on and Lydgate was surprised that he had heard nothing from the agent, Mr Trumbull.

'I must go to see him again,' he said to Rosamond, as they were having breakfast. 'I'll tell him to advertise the house in the local papers.'

'I told Trumbull that we were not moving,' Rosamond said calmly. 'I told him not to do anything.'

Lydgate stared at his wife in amazement.

'When and why did you do that?' he asked in surprise.

Money Matters

'The same day that you went to see him,' Rosamond replied. 'I knew that it would be a mistake to move. I did not want to,' she added with a smile.

'Can't I make you understand my situation at all?' Lydgate asked angrily. 'Don't you ever listen when I speak to you?'

'I have a right to speak too,' Rosamond replied coldly.

'But only to me, not to other people,' Lydgate told her.

'You did not speak to me like this before I married you,' Rosamond said. 'Everyone told me that you were doing so well. I did not know that you had all these problems.'

'The problems came *after* the marriage,' Lydgate replied. 'You must be able to see that.'

Rosamond did not reply at once. Then, after some time, she said,

'Don't forget that we are dining at Papa's tonight, Tertius. I hope you will be in a better mood by then.'

Two weeks went by and there were more bills to pay. Lydgate was in despair.

'I shall have to ask my uncle to help me,' he thought at last. 'It is no good sending a letter. I shall have to travel north and see him myself.'

Then, a few days later, after Lydgate had gone out, a letter came from Sir Godwin. Rosamond was delighted. The letter was addressed to her husband, but that did not worry her.

'That means it is good news,' Rosamond said to herself. 'Of course, he is sending the money to Tertius, not me.'

When Lydgate arrived home, Rosamond ran up to him with the letter in her hand.

'There is a letter for you, Tertius,' she cried. 'Do open it quickly!'

'It's from my uncle Godwin!' Lydgate said in surprise.

He opened the letter quickly, read it and then threw it on the table.

Money Matters

'How can I go on living with you after this?' he said.
Rosamond picked up the letter.

Dear Tertius,

An honest man does not get his wife to write begging letters for him. You ask for one thousand pounds, but that is impossible. I have five children and no money to spare.

I might have helped you, if you had gone into the army or the Church. You chose medicine and seem to have made a mess of it. I can't help you and the sooner you go somewhere else, the better.

I wish you well, but you must solve your own problems.

Your loving uncle,

Godwin Lydgate

'Now do you see what trouble you are making?' Lydgate asked his wife. 'Why must you do things without asking me first?'

Rosamond did not answer, but a tear ran down her face.

'There is no one to help me now,' she said. 'I have always done what is right. Why do you blame me? Marriage has made me so unhappy. I wish that I had died with the baby.'

Then her tears began to fall and her husband knew that there was nothing he could say or do to change her mind. He sat down beside her and, very gently, took her in his arms.

16

Temptation

There was only one man in Middlemarch who was unhappier than Doctor Lydgate. That man was Nicholas Bulstrode. He had given John Raffles money to leave Middlemarch, but Raffles had come back, not once, but several times.

Raffles now had a room of his own at Stone Court where he could meet Bulstrode in secret. But Raffles also spent a lot of time drinking in Middlemarch. He listened to the gossip of the town too and he soon heard a name that he recognized.

That name was Ladislaw.

'Well, Nick, that was a surprise,' Raffles said when he saw Bulstrode again. 'Ladislaw is a Polish name, I believe. I had heard it before and you know it too. I have found out that a young man called Will Ladislaw is living in Middlemarch. He is Sarah Dunkirk's son and your money really belongs to him. Are you going to do anything to put that right, Nick? Perhaps I should speak to young Ladislaw about it. Yes I think I will. Or maybe I'll just tell him that I knew his mother in London. That will interest him, won't it, Nick?'

Bulstrode did not answer. This proud, cold man gave away money in the hope that people would respect him. He went to church to show everyone how good he was. He had almost forgotten the sins[96] of his past life, but now Raffles had made him think about them again. Bulstrode was terrified of being found out and his fear began to make him ill.

'I cannot live like this any longer,' Bulstrode said to himself, a few days later. 'I shall have to leave Middlemarch. I have been here for nearly thirty years and the people here respect me. But all that will change if they find out about my past. I will do anything to stop that happening – anything.'

Temptation

Bulstrode decided that Ladislaw must be told the truth. He wrote a letter to the young man, asking to meet him on business. Will agreed, thinking that Bulstrode wanted to talk about the *Pioneer*.

'What is the matter? You don't look well,' Will said when he came into the room.

'Please sit down, Mr Ladislaw,' Bulstrode replied. 'What I have to say must remain a secret between us. It is something that concerns us both. It is a family matter, Mr Ladislaw.'

Will said nothing.

'I believe that your mother's name was Sarah Dunkirk. And that she left her family to become an actress,' Mr Bulstrode said. His was voice shaking.

'Yes, that is true,' Will replied.

'Did she ever mention her mother to you?' Bulstrode asked.

'She loved her and pitied her,' Will said quickly.

Bulstrode sighed. 'Sarah's mother, your grandmother, became my wife,' he said. 'That marriage made me a rich man, Mr Ladislaw, and left your mother poor. I should have searched London for her, but I did not. That was a sin – a sin for which I ask forgiveness.'

'My mother has been dead for some time,' Will said coldly.

'Then now I must help her son,' Bulstrode said. 'I am willing to give you five hundred pounds a year while I am alive.'

Will Ladislaw stood up and walked away from the banker.

'My mother knew her family's money was made in a dishonourable way,' Will said in an angry voice. 'That was why she ran away. My honour is as important to me as my mother's was to her – so I refuse to take a penny of your dirty money. We have nothing more to say to each other, Mr Bulstrode. Goodbye.'

―――

January and February of the new year had passed and it was now March. Doctor Lydgate felt depressed and hopeless. Rosamond had twice asked her father to help them, but he had refused.

'It has been a bad year for trade and I have no money to spare,'

Temptation

Mr Vincy said. 'Why doesn't your husband ask Bulstrode? Bankers always have plenty of money and Lydgate sees him at the New Hospital nearly every day.'

Lydgate had been thinking about asking Bulstrode for a loan for some time.

'I have done a lot of work for him at the New Hospital,' Lydgate said to himself. 'That has stopped me making my practice[97] bigger. So, in a way, Bulstrode owes me the money. Shall I write to him? No, I'll go to see him myself.'

But the next day, a note came from Mr Bulstrode, asking Lydgate to see him at the bank.

'I have not been sleeping well lately,' Bulstrode told the doctor. 'My health is not good. If cholera comes to the town, I could be in danger.'

'You are not strong, I agree,' Lydgate said. 'Perhaps you spend too much time here at the bank.'

'I'm sure you are right,' Bulstrode replied. 'And all my work at the New Hospital has become a problem too. I can no longer afford to give it my time or my money. We tried to do too much there, I think, Doctor Lydgate.'

'That will be a great loss to the New Hospital,' Lydgate said sadly.

'Well, the New Hospital can be joined to the old one,' Bulstrode said. 'The doctors there will work with you, I'm sure.'

'But their ideas are different from mine. They refuse to do things in the modern way,' Lydgate replied. 'I shall have no control over the work at all.'

'I'm sorry to disappoint you,' Bulstrode said, 'but I may be leaving Middlemarch soon, for health reasons. However, I think that Mrs Casaubon may have good news for you. She is a wealthy woman and she wishes to help the hospital in any way she can. Ask her, Doctor Lydgate. Ask her.'

'I will,' Lydgate replied. 'Thank you for telling me all this. My work at the New Hospital has been very important to me, but it has stopped me from getting more patients. And the ones that I have are often too poor to pay me.'

Bulstrode said nothing, but he shook his head sadly.

'I want to tell you that I have many debts,' Lydgate went on. 'I need a thousand pounds to pay them all. You are the only person I can ask to help me. You know how hard I have worked to help this town.'

'I am sorry to hear of your problem, but I am not surprised,' Bulstrode said. 'The Vincys have always been careless with money. You did not make a good marriage and now you must suffer for your mistake. I advise you to become a bankrupt[98], Mr Lydgate. There is no other way.'

'Thank you,' said Lydgate, standing up. 'I am sorry to have wasted your time. Good day, Mr Bulstrode. Good day.'

When Mrs Bulstrode heard about Lydgate's debts, she was very upset.

'You have always been very hard on my family, Nicholas,' she said to her husband. 'Surely you can help poor Rosamond now. My niece is such a sweet girl, you know.'

'My dear Harriet,' Bulstrode replied. 'I have given your brother a good deal of money in the past. You cannot expect me to take care of his married children too.'

But very soon something happened that made him change his mind.

17

The Secret is Out

The next afternoon, Bulstrode had another visitor at the Bank. It was his farm-manager, Caleb Garth.

'I have just come from Stone Court, Mr Bulstrode,' Garth said slowly.

'There's nothing wrong with the farm, I hope,' Bulstrode replied.

'No, but you have a man staying in the house from time to time. He told me his name is John Raffles. I have seen him in Middlemarch too. He is very ill and he needs a doctor,' Garth said.

'Thank you for telling me,' Bulstrode said quickly. 'I shall send a servant to find Doctor Lydgate. Then I shall go to Stone Court myself.'

Bulstrode stood up, but Garth did not move.

'Raffles has told me a lot more than his name,' the farm-manager said. 'He has told me a great deal about you. He has told me how you made your money. I am sorry, Mr Bulstrode, but I cannot work for you any longer. You have done too many bad things.'

'Do you believe everything that Raffles has told you?' Bulstrode cried. 'Let me know what he has said to you!'

Garth shook his head. 'No,' he said. 'I am sure that Raffles is telling the truth. There is no need to say any more.'

'Then promise me that you will not tell anything of this to anyone else,' Bulstrode said.

'I can promise that,' Garth replied. 'But Raffles has been talking about you to people in Middlemarch too. I am not the only man to know these stories. Goodbye, Mr Bulstrode.'

The Secret is Out

As soon as Caleb Garth had left, Bulstrode got on his horse and rode quickly to Stone Court. He was very shocked when he saw Raffles. He looked ill and weak and he could not speak clearly.

Soon afterwards, Lydgate arrived and he examined Raffles carefully.

'He is seriously ill, I think,' Bulstrode said to the doctor.

'Not seriously, perhaps. But he needs looking after. Is he a friend of yours?

'Not a friend. He used to work for me,' Bulstrode replied quickly. 'But I feel sorry for him. I shall stay here and look after him myself.'

Lydgate was surprised, but he said,

'Very well. I shall give you my instructions. This man has been drinking a good deal and his mind is very confused. Try to keep him quiet and warm. He has been asking for brandy, but do not give it to him. Any more alcohol will kill him. I shall come to see him again tomorrow.'

Then Lydgate bowed and left.

'Bulstrode is a strange man,' Lydgate said to himself as he rode his horse back to Middlemarch. 'He refuses to help his family, but he is willing to help this stranger from his past. I will have to tell Rosy that her uncle will not lend us the money. I do not know what else I can do now.'

When Lydgate got home, he found that things had got worse. There was a bailiff[99] in the house, who would stay there until the debts were paid.

Rosamond was crying in her bedroom. When Lydgate saw his wife's unhappiness, he began to cry too.

'Forgive me, Rosy. There is nothing more I can do,' he said.

'Papa will not help us,' Rosamond replied. 'But he says that I can stay with them until all this is over. I shall go tomorrow.'

Lydgate was suddenly very angry.

The Secret is Out

'Oh, wait a day or two,' he shouted. 'I may fall off my horse and break my neck. Then you will have the money from my life insurance!'

'If you do not want me to go, say so,' Rosamond said coldly. 'I shall stay if you wish it. You do not have to shout.'

'I do wish it,' Lydgate replied. 'But now I have work to do. I cannot stop seeing my patients. You may not need me, but they do.'

The next day, Lydgate returned to Stone Court to see Raffles again. The old man had been awake all night, talking and shouting. Bulstrode was terrified of Raffles now and, in his heart, Bulstrode wished that Raffles would die.

Lydgate looked at Raffles and examined him carefully.

'He is worse,' the doctor said. 'All the alcohol he has drunk is killing him. But I may be able to do something. Are you staying here to look after him?'

'Yes,' Bulstrode replied. 'My housekeeper will be here too. What must we do?'

'I have brought some opium[100], to make him sleep,' Lydgate said. 'Give him very small doses until the exact time I have written down here. Don't give him any more after that. And no alcohol. No alcohol at all. Then we can hope that he may recover.'

'Thank you. You look ill yourself, Lydgate,' Bulstrode said. 'You have many problems, I know.'

'I have,' Lydgate said. 'They are getting worse, day by day.'

'I have thought again about this and I think that I may be able to help you,' Bulstrode said slowly. 'My wife is worried about her niece. And you have done much good work for this town. I would like that to go on. I will write you a cheque for one thousand pounds. I think you said that would pay your debts?'

'Yes, yes,' Lydgate said in a shocked voice. 'That would solve my problems and allow me to do my work as I should.'

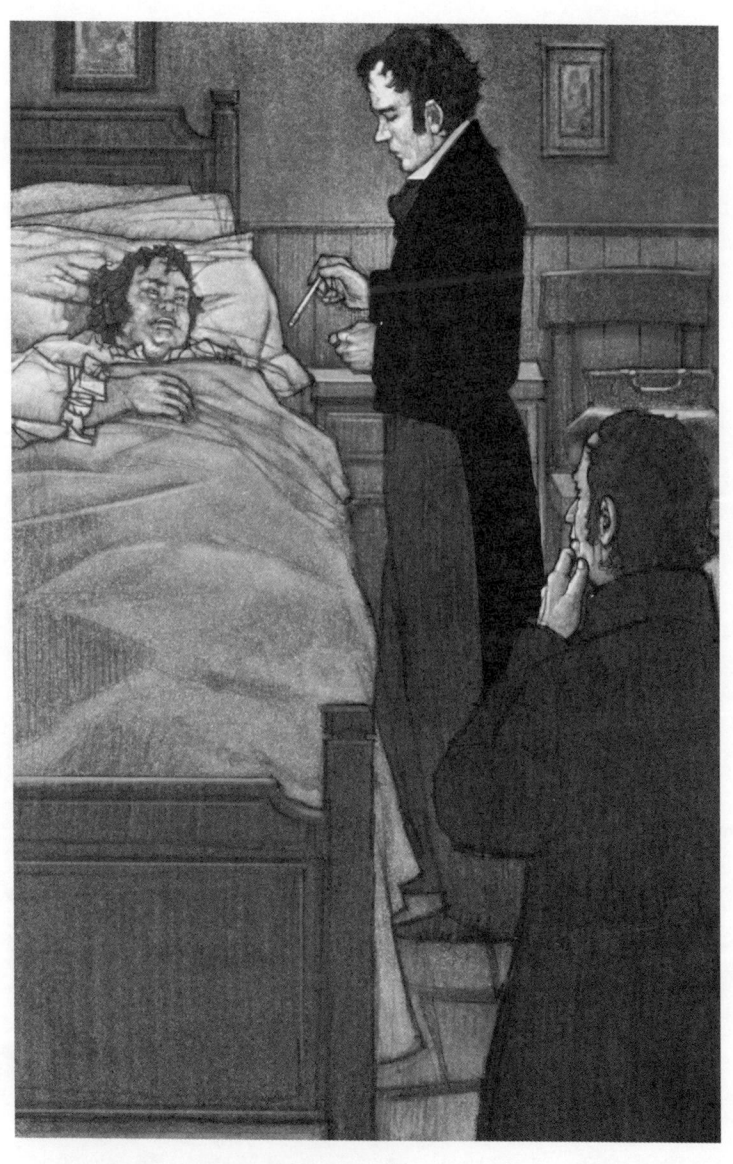

*Lydgate looked at Raffles and examined him carefully.
'He is worse,' the doctor said.*

The Secret is Out

'Then I shall write you a cheque at once,' the banker said, 'You can pay me back when you are able to.'

Lydgate thanked Bulstrode as he took the cheque. The young doctor felt happy for the first time in many months. He thanked Bulstrode again and then hurried home to tell Rosamond the good news.

Bulstrode had been awake most of the night and he was now very tired. He called his housekeeper, Mrs Abel, and carefully gave her Lydgate's instructions about the doses of opium.

'Will he want anything else, sir?' Mrs Abel asked.

'Perhaps some soup, if he asks for it,' Bulstrode replied. 'Nothing else.'

He went to his room, but could not sleep. Then he remembered that he had not told Mrs Abel when to stop giving Raffles the opium.

'But he can't come to any harm,' Bulstrode said to himself. 'Lydgate did not leave enough opium for that.'

Some time later, there was a knock on his bedroom door.

'What is it, Mrs Abel?' Bulstrode said as he saw his housekeeper.

'The poor man is feeling worse,' Mrs Abel began. 'He won't eat anything, but he says that he would like a little brandy. When I was nursing my last master, the doctor told me to give him brandy, whenever he wanted it. Can't I give some to Mr Raffles, sir?'

Bulstrode did not reply.

'I'm sure the brandy won't harm him, sir,' Mrs Abel went on. 'There is plenty in the cupboard downstairs, sir and you don't drink it yourself.'

Again Bulstrode was silent. Then he took a key from his pocket.

'That is the key to the cupboard, Mrs Abel,' he said. 'Give Mr Raffles what he wants.'

The Secret is Out

Early the next morning, Bulstrode went to Raffles' bedroom.

'He's asleep, sir,' Mrs Abel whispered.

'Then you go to your room and rest, Mrs Abel. I shall look after Mr Raffles now,' Bulstrode said.

He went into Raffles' room and shut the door behind him. One look at the bed told him the truth. Raffles was alive, but his sleep was the sleep that would end in death.

The opium was nearly all gone. Bulstrode put it in his pocket. He picked up the half-empty brandy bottle, took it downstairs with him and locked it in the cupboard.

When Lydgate returned, later in the morning, Raffles was dead. The doctor was surprised, but he did not ask Bulstrode any questions.

Lydgate and Bulstrode rode back into Middlemarch together in silence. But if the two men were hoping for a better life in the future, they were wrong. Raffles had spoken to too many people in the town and everyone had heard his stories about Bulstrode. Now everyone began to turn against the banker. Then people started to say that Raffles had died very suddenly – far too suddenly – when he was staying at Stone Court.

The gossip had started and soon it began to grow and grow. No one in Middlemarch had ever liked Bulstrode. He had always thought himself better than other people. Now those people had a chance to make him look very bad indeed.

Then someone found out that Bulstrode had lent Lydgate money to pay his debts. Lydgate had been called to Stone Court several times and yet Raffles had died. So the young doctor's modern ideas did not work after all! Or perhaps the money had been a bribe[101]. Had Lydgate done Bulstrode a favour? People began to gossip about Lydgate too. He had not been born in Middlemarch and neither had Bulstrode. The people of Middlemarch decided that they did not need strangers to look after their business.

A meeting had been planned about public health in the Town Hall and this gave Bulstrode's enemies their chance to let the

The Secret is Out

banker know what they thought of him. When the room was full, a man stood up and began to speak.

'Before we discuss the health of this town and the possibility of cholera, there is another matter to be decided,' he said. 'That matter concerns Mr Nicholas Bulstrode. And it concerns justice!

'Mr Bulstrode came to Middlemarch as a stranger, many years ago and we trusted him. Now, at last, we have heard the truth about his past. We have heard about his dishonesty and meanness! A man has died in Mr Bulstrode's house. The same man who had told us the truth about Nicholas Bulstrode! Mr Bulstrode holds several important official positions in Middlemarch. For the good of the town, we ask him to resign[102] from these positions at once!'

Everyone cheered. Bulstrode himself stood up and tried to speak. His face was white and he was shaking with anger and fear. Lydgate stood up quickly and went towards Bulstrode.

'You are ill. Let me take you home,' he said quietly.

The two men left the meeting in silence. Then, as the door closed behind them, everyone cheered.

Mr Brooke had been at the meeting in the Town Hall and he was very surprised by what had happened. He had not heard the gossip, but someone soon told him. Mr Brooke did not know much about the Mr Bulstrode, the banker, but he believed that Lydgate was a good doctor.

Dorothea, who had just returned from a trip to the north, was back at Lowick Manor. Her uncle decided to drive there at once and Dorothea was delighted to see him.

'I have bad news, I'm afraid, my dear, very bad news,' Mr Brooke said at once.

'What is the matter, Uncle?' Dorothea cried. 'Are you ill?'

'No, not at all,' Mr Brooke replied. 'I have just come from a meeting in the Town Hall. A meeting about public health, you know. There is a fear of cholera coming to Middlemarch and we must be prepared.'

'Then I suppose Doctor Lydgate was there and Mr Bulstrode too, I expect,' Dorothea said. 'I have agreed to help them with the New Hospital and now we should begin planning at once. If we are ready to fight the cholera, then that is good news, not bad.'

'The bad news is about Bulstrode and Lydgate,' Mr Brooke said. 'I am afraid that they have both behaved very badly, very badly indeed.'

Dorothea listened to her uncle in silence as he told her all he knew. Then she shook her head.

'I don't know very much about Mr Bulstrode,' she said, 'but I do know Doctor Lydgate. He has not done anything wrong, I am sure of that. Let us find out the truth about him and clear his name!'

18

Two Wives

Lydgate now cursed the day that he had come to Middlemarch. Everything had gone wrong – his work, his marriage, his whole life. Lydgate wished too that he had never taken the cheque from Bulstrode.

Lydgate could not return the money because he had used it to pay his debts and he soon realized that people were linking his name with Bulstrode's. The people of Middlemarch began to avoid the young doctor and several of them stopped being his patients.

'How can I explain all this to Rosy?' Lydgate thought. 'She will never understand and she will blame me for everything.'

Dorothea was convinced that Lydgate had done nothing wrong, but her family told her to be careful.

Two Wives

'Lydgate must manage his own life. You can't do it for him,' Sir James said. 'He took money from Bulstrode and Bulstrode cannot be trusted,' he went on. 'We must wait a little and see what happens.'

'Yes, Dorothea dear,' Celia said. 'Sir James is right. You always do things without thinking. You obeyed Mr Casaubon. Now listen to my husband. Men know all about money and business. Women don't.'

'I obeyed Mr Casaubon because he was my husband,' Dorothea said. 'Now I have no husband, I want to think for myself again! My money is my own and I want to use it to help the New Hospital. I have so many ideas for making it better. There is nothing wrong with that, I suppose.'

'Of course not, my dear,' Mr Brooke said calmly. 'But you must be careful, you know. I have spent a great deal on my estate and so has Sir James. Do wait a little and think carefully before you spend your money too!'

Rosamond Lydgate and Harriet Bulstrode found out about their husbands' troubles in different ways.

Mrs Bulstrode had been very upset when Lydgate brought her husband home from the meeting in the Town Hall.

'Is my husband ill?' Harriet Bulstrode asked. 'He looks very pale.'

'The room was very crowded. It was difficult to breathe,' Lydgate replied. 'I expect Mr Bulstrode has been working too hard.'

Mrs Bulstrode was afraid to ask her husband anything and he stayed in his room for four days. No one called at the house during that time and Mrs Bulstrode knew that something must be wrong.

On the fifth day, Mrs Bulstrode drove to her brother's warehouse, to ask Mr Vincy what had happened.

'God help you, Harriet,' Mr Vincy said when he saw his sister. 'I see that you know everything.'

Two Wives

Mrs Vincy went very pale and sat down. 'You are wrong, brother. I know nothing,' she whispered. 'Tell me the truth, please. Nicholas has said nothing to me at all.'

So Mr Vincy told her all he knew.

'Nothing can be proved,' he said at last. 'But people will talk, whether the gossip is true or not and I am afraid it is. I wish that you and Rosamond had never married, Harriet. I wish that you had both kept the name of Vincy all your lives.'

Harriet Bulstrode went home straight away and knocked on the door of her husband's room. Bulstrode was sitting at his desk. His wife went up to him and put her hands on his shoulders.

'I know everything, Nicholas,' she said.

Then Bulstrode began to cry and his wife sat down beside him and cried too. Despite everything he had done, she had married him and she would forgive him. There was nothing more to say.

When all the debts had been paid, Rosamond felt happier for a time. But, as Lydgate had thought, she blamed her husband for their problems and she now hated living in Middlemarch.

'Will Ladislaw left, why can't I?' Rosamond asked herself. 'I wish that I had married him and not Tertius. I am sure that Will prefers me to Mrs Casaubon. But now all I have are the letters he writes to us. Tertius and I must go to live in London.' Rosamond smiled. 'Then Will can visit us there and sing and flirt with me, as he did before,' she thought.

In his next letter to the Lydgates, Will wrote that he was planning a visit to Middlemarch. All at once, Rosamond was happy again.

Then Rosamond realised that she had not entertained their neighbours for some time. Without telling her husband, she sent out invitations for a small evening party. But to her surprise, no one could come.

When Lydgate found out about the invitations, he was very angry.

'Why did you send out all those invitations without asking me first?' he cried. 'I could have told you that no one would come.'

Rosamond said nothing.

'Do you hear me?' Lydgate shouted.

'You are shouting, Tertius. Of course I can hear you,' his wife replied, turning her head away. She did not say anything more, but later that day, she called on her parents.

Mr and Mrs Vincy were sitting together and when Mr Vincy saw his daughter, he shook his head and sighed.

'Is there anything the matter, Papa?' Rosamond asked quickly.

'Oh, my dear,' Mrs Vincy said. 'Haven't you heard about your uncle Bulstrode? Debt was bad enough, but this will be worse.'

'What do you mean?' Rosamond said.

So her father told her everything.

'I think that Lydgate must leave the town,' he said at last. 'He may not have done wrong, but everyone here is against him now.'

This was a terrible shock to Rosamond, but she went home quietly and said nothing to her husband. Lydgate knew that when his wife was quiet, she was hiding something. He guessed at once what had happened.

'What have you heard?' Lydgate asked.

'Everything. Papa told me.'

Lydgate waited for some words of love and support from his wife, but none came.

'Tertius,' she said at last. 'I cannot live in Middlemarch now. Let us go to London. It will be easier for me there.'

Lydgate did not reply and a few minutes later, he walked out of the house.

'Tertius doesn't realize how terrible this is for me,' Rosamond said to herself, 'but Will is coming back soon. I'll tell him everything. *He* will understand.'

19
Dorothea Makes Some Decisions

A few days later, Dorothea asked Lydgate to visit her at Lowick Manor. The big house, with its beautiful gardens, was a restful place, but Dorothea was very unhappy.

'I have too much money,' she said to herself. 'How can I be happy here, when poor people need so much? The New Hospital must go on and with my money and Doctor Lydgate's help, it will.'

But when she saw Lydgate, Dorothea was shocked by the change in him. He had the face of a man who had lost all hope.

'I understand that you want to help the New Hospital, Mrs Casaubon,' Lydgate said. 'But I have to tell you that I may have to leave Middlemarch. I suppose that you have heard why.'

'I have not heard anything that has changed my opinion of you,' Dorothea said sweetly. 'Why don't you tell me the true story, Doctor Lydgate? Your name can be cleared, I am sure. Let me help you to do it.'

So the young doctor told Dorothea everything. He told her about his debts, the death of Raffles and the money from Bulstrode.

'We could do so much good for the town, if you stayed,' Dorothea said gently. 'In time, all those things would be forgotten, I'm sure of it.'

'Mrs Casaubon, there is something else,' Lydgate said at last. 'I am married. You know what that means. I cannot think only of myself. My wife is very unhappy and she wants to leave. Our marriage has brought her so much trouble and she refuses to talk to me about it.'

Dorothea Makes Some Decisions

'May I go and see her?' Dorothea asked. 'Would she listen to me? I did meet her once. I remember that she was very pretty.'

'I am sure that she would see you. But I don't think that she would change her mind. And I am not sure whether I have the strength to go on here in Middlemarch. It might be better for us to leave.'

'It is not brave to give up the fight,' Dorothea replied.

'Perhaps not,' Lydgate said. 'But anyhow, I am sure that Rosy would like to see you before we leave.'

'Then I will visit her,' Dorothea said with a smile.

After Lydgate had gone, Dorothea made her decision. She wrote him a cheque for one thousand pounds and put it in an envelope with a short note. This way, Lydgate would owe her the money, rather than Bulstrode.

'I shall take the cheque with me tomorrow,' Dorothea said to herself.

The next day, Dorothea ordered her carriage and drove into Middlemarch to see Rosamond Lydgate. The last time they had met, Will Ladislaw had been there too.

Dorothea allowed herself to think of Will from time to time, with a mixture of pleasure and pain. There had been strong feeling between them at their last meeting, but marriage was, of course, impossible.

Dorothea stopped the carriage opposite the Lydgates' house and got out. The door of the house was open and a servant was standing there, looking at the grand carriage.

'Is Mrs Lydgate at home?' Dorothea asked. 'I am Mrs Casaubon.'

She followed the maid, who opened the door of the sitting-room without looking in. Dorothea entered the room quietly. She heard voices and then she saw Will Ladislaw and Rosamond Lydgate sitting closely together on the couch. Rosamond's face

She saw Will Ladislaw and Rosamund Lydgate sitting closely together on the couch.

Dorothea Makes Some Decisions

was covered with tears. Will was talking to Rosamond and holding her hands in his.

At the terrible shock of seeing them together, Dorothea stepped back quickly and hit a piece of furniture with her foot. Rosamond looked up at the noise and saw her. As Rosamond stood up, Will turned round and saw Dorothea too.

Dorothea was the first to speak.

'Excuse me, Mrs Lydgate,' she said clearly. 'The servant did not know you were here. I have brought an important letter for Doctor Lydgate. I'll leave it on this table.'

Dorothea put down the letter, bowed and hurried from the room. In a few minutes more, she was in her carriage and driving away.

Will and Rosamond stood in silence, looking at the open door. Then Rosamond smiled and put her little white hand on Will's arm.

'Don't touch me!' he shouted, moving away to the other side of the room.

He stood there, with his hands in his pockets, not looking at her at all.

Rosamond sat down and spoke very quietly,

'Why don't you go after Mrs Casaubon and tell her how you feel?' she said. 'It is quite clear that you prefer her to me.'

'You have no idea how I feel,' Will replied angrily. 'How can you, when you think of no one but yourself? Go after her? How can I? She will never look at me again.'

'You find it easy to explain your feelings to me,' Rosamond said coldly. 'Explain them to her!'

'Then I must explain that I am a man in hell,' Will cried. 'And I don't "prefer" Mrs Casaubon. There is no other woman in the world for me except her!'

No one had ever spoken to Rosamond like this before. She closed her eyes and sat completely still.

Dorothea Makes Some Decisions

Then Will suddenly realized the truth. Rosamond wanted love, not friendship, from him. She was sure that she could always get what she wanted. She could not believe that Will loved Dorothea and not her.

'I must go now,' Will said at last. 'I shall come back tonight to see Lydgate.'

'If you like,' Rosamond replied, without opening her eyes.

When Lydgate returned, Rosamond was crying on her bed.

'My poor Rosamond! What has upset you?' he cried. And he took her in his arms and kissed her.

Will called again in the evening, but he did not tell Lydgate that he had been in the house that morning. Rosamond was upstairs and Lydgate told Will the whole story of himself, Bulstrode and John Raffles.

'I believe that Raffles spoke to you too,' Lydgate said. 'Much of Bulstrode's money belongs to you.'

'I did hear the story,' Will said quietly. 'But I know how Bulstrode made that money. It was done in a shameful way and it would be shameful of me, Sarah Dunkirk's son, to try to claim it. I would rather stay poor all my life. Please let us not speak of it again.'

Then Will bowed to his friend and left the house quickly. He did not want to tell Lydgate that Bulstrode had offered him money and that he had refused it. Lydgate had accepted a loan from the banker and Will did not wish his friend to blame himself for doing so.

'Lydgate is in debt and I am not,' Will said to himself when he was alone. 'Of course, I need money, but I must make it for myself, if I can. But Dorothea's family will never see me as her equal. Never, never.'

Tertius Lydgate and Will Ladislaw were both young men, but neither of them could think of the future with any hope of happiness.

Dorothea Makes Some Decisions

Dorothea spent the rest of the day at Freshitt Hall. When she returned home in the evening, she was very tired. Telling her maid that she wanted to be alone, Dorothea went to her bedroom and locked the door.

At last she began to cry. 'Oh, I did love him,' she whispered. 'How I loved him! I thought that he was worthy of my love and I trusted him. What did I know of love before I met Will Ladislaw? He came into my dark world like a bright light and awoke me from my sleeping half-life. He made me feel more deeply than I had ever felt before and then, then he deceived me. He knew that I had no experience of love and he made me believe his lies. I hate him for that now, I hate and despise him. Why did he say those things to me when he loved Rosamond Lydgate? I have seen them together now and I know that is true. She is false to her marriage and Will is false to me.'

At last Dorothea cried herself to sleep. But when she woke up, some hours later, her thoughts were clearer.

'I must not think only of myself,' she said. 'There are three other people whose lives may be saved too. What is the right thing for me to do? How can I put things right for them? I must do what is right, I must.'

Dorothea sighed. 'I must forget Will now and try to help Rosamond,' she said out loud. 'I will go to Middlemarch tomorrow and speak to her again. Perhaps I can help to save her marriage.'

20

True Conversations

Dorothea walked into Middlemarch the next morning. She arrived as Lydgate was leaving the house.

'Do you think that Mrs Lydgate can see me this morning?' Dorothea said.

'I am sure she will,' Lydgate replied. Then he took a letter from his pocket and put it into Dorothea's hand.

'I was planning to ride to Lowick to give you this, with my deepest thanks,' he said.

'I must thank *you* for letting me help you,' Dorothea replied.

Lydgate bowed. 'I will tell Mrs Lydgate that you are here in the sitting-room,' he said.

Rosamond dared not refuse to see Dorothea, but she did not know why she had returned. She went downstairs slowly, walked into the sitting-room and bowed to her visitor. But Dorothea held out her hand and Rosamond took it in hers. The two women sat down, facing each other. Both of them were very pale.

'I would like to talk to you about your husband, if you will let me,' Dorothea began.

Rosamond smiled sadly. 'I know you have been very good to him,' she said.

'Mr Lydgate has told me the whole story,' Dorothea explained. 'People have said bad things about him, but he has done nothing wrong. I am sure of that and I have told my family so. They believe in your husband too. That makes you feel happier, doesn't it?'

'Thank you. You are very kind,' Rosamond replied. Her blue eyes filled with tears.

'Trouble is hard to bear alone,' Dorothea went on. 'When someone we love is in trouble, we must help them. You know that, of course. It may be very difficult, but we must always try.'

True Conversations

Dorothea was talking about her own troubles as well as Rosamond's, but it was Rosamond who began to cry.

'Your husband blames himself for not talking to you,' Dorothea said, bowing her head. 'But his feelings for you are very strong. Marriage is such a close relationship, isn't it? I have known how difficult it can be. We may have other strong feelings – I have also had such feelings – feelings that have taken hold of me. And I am weak, too weak to let them go...'

Dorothea's face was very white and she could say no more. For perhaps the first time in her life, Rosamond was not thinking about herself. She leaned forward and kissed Dorothea gently on the forehead. Then she said,

'What you are thinking is not true. When you came yesterday, Will was telling me that he loved another woman – that he has never loved me. He said yesterday that you were the only woman who existed for him. And now I think that he hates me, because you did not understand what you saw yesterday. There, that is the truth and I'm glad that I've told you.'

Dorothea's own happiness was now almost too strong to bear. But she made herself think about Rosamond and not herself.

'Better times will come for you and your husband. He depends on you for comfort and he loves you very much,' Dorothea said.

'Tertius did not blame me then?' Rosamond asked.

'No, of course not,' Dorothea replied. At that moment, the door opened and Lydgate came into the room.

'I am here as your doctor,' he said with a smile. 'When I went away, I could not forget your two pale faces. I noticed you were walking Mrs Casaubon. May I send for your carriage? I think it may rain.'

'Oh, no, I am strong. I need the exercise,' Dorothea replied. 'It is time for me to go. Goodbye, Mrs Lydgate, and thank you for listening to me.'

When Dorothea had gone, Lydgate returned to his wife with a smile.

True Conversations

'Well, Rosy,' he said. 'What do you think of Mrs Casaubon now?'

'She is very good and very beautiful, Tertius,' Rosamond replied. 'You will soon like her better than me.'

Lydgate laughed. Then he said, 'But has she made you happier with me, Rosy?'

Rosamond looked up at her husband's face. Then she lifted a hand and brushed back his hair.

'I think she has Tertius,' she replied softly. 'I think she has.'

Will Ladislaw called at the Lydgates that evening. He had come back to Middlemarch to see Dorothea, to talk to her again and explain his true feelings for her. But Dorothea had seen him with Rosamond Lydgate and now his hope was crushed.

Both Rosamond and Will had things to say to each other, but they could not speak in front of Tertius Lydgate. He stayed in the room all evening.

When Rosamond poured out Will's tea, he stood up to fetch it. She had put a little note in the saucer and he put it in his pocket quickly.

When he was back at the inn where he was staying, Will read the note.

> *I have told Mrs Casaubon. She came to see me and she was very kind. I have not spoilt anything for you. I have told her how you feel. She knows the truth now.*

Will did not know whether he was happy or sad. What had Rosamond said to Dorothea? What did Dorothea think of him now? Would they ever have the chance to talk to each other again?

Will wanted these questions answered. But he dared not guess what those answers would be.

21
After the Storm

After her visit to Rosamond, Dorothea had two nights of good sleep. She felt full of life again. She spent most of the first day walking in her gardens. On the second day, she tried to find something useful to do.

The poor people in the village were well and happy – there was nothing to do there. Dorothea thought about visiting her uncle at Tipton Grange, but decided to stay at home.

'I need to read more,' Dorothea thought to herself. 'I'll stay in the library today.'

But she could not find a book to interest her. She was looking at one of the paintings on the wall, when the door opened quietly. It was Will Ladislaw.

'I told your butler not to announce me,' Will said. 'I thought that you might not want to see me,'

He walked very slowly towards Dorothea, who was standing completely still.

'Of course I wanted to see you,' she said.

'I had to explain something to you,' Will said. 'You know my family history and how I am known to Mr Bulstrode. He offered me money, but I refused to take it.'

'You did right, as you always do,' Dorothea replied.

'My life has no meaning now and I can never be happy,' Will said. 'But I have always been true to you and I always shall be. I want you to know that.'

'I do know it,' Dorothea said, holding out her hand.

Will took her hand and kissed it. Then Dorothea turned and moved away to the window.

'How dark the clouds are!' she said. 'And the wind is becoming stronger too. There is going to be a storm.'

After the Storm

Will stepped a little nearer to her. They stood in silence, not looking at each other, but at the gardens outside. The trees were moving in the strong wind and the sky was black. The thunder was nearer now. Suddenly, there was a flash of lightning, which startled them both and made them look at each other.

'It was wrong to say that you can never be happy,' Dorothea whispered. 'I have felt great sadness too. Perhaps it has made me stronger. You will grow stronger too, even... even without...'

'We have been able to see each other for one last time,' Will said. 'Think of me sometimes. But you must think of me as a dead man.'

Another bright flash of lightning lit up the darkened room. Dorothea ran from the window in fear. Will followed her and held her hands. The storm was over the house now and the thunder shook the room. As the rain began to pour down, they looked into each others' eyes for the first time.

'There is no hope for me,' Will said. 'Even if you loved me as I love you, I would still be poor. It is impossible for us to be together. I should not have come. I am sorry.'

'Don't be sorry,' Dorothea said. 'I...'

She could not speak. They moved towards each other again and kissed for the first time.

The rain was still falling against the windows and the wind was blowing strongly. Inside the library, there was silence. Dorothea sat down on a couch in the middle of the room. Will sat down beside her and held her hand. They sat until the rain stopped falling and everything outside was quiet too.

'Oh, it is impossible!' Will cried. 'We love each other, but we can never be married!'

'Some time, we might...' Dorothea began.

'Some time? When?' Will asked angrily. 'No. People would always say that I ruined your life.' Then he stood up and reached for his hat. 'I must go,' he said quickly. 'Goodbye.'

'Oh I cannot bear it, my heart is breaking!' Dorothea cried,

'Oh I cannot bear it, my heart is breaking!' Dorothea cried.

After the Storm

rising from her seat. Tears began to pour down her cheeks. 'You must not go. I cannot bear it! I don't mind about being poor. I hate my husband's money. I hate it!'

Immediately Will put his arms around her.

'I have some money of my own,' she said. 'We could live quite well on that. I shall not want anything for myself. We have each other! Nothing else matters now.'

The next day was fine. At Freshitt Hall, Celia was sitting in the flower garden, playing with her baby, little Arthur. Her husband, Sir James Chettam, was reading the London newspaper. Everything was peaceful and quiet.

Celia looked up.

'Oh, look. Here is my uncle,' she said. Leaving the baby with his nurse, Celia ran towards Mr Brooke and held his arm.

'Sad news, sad news, my dear,' Mr Brooke said.

Sir James looked up from his newspaper. 'What's the matter?' he said. 'You are talking about politics, I suppose. I'm reading the news from London now.'

'No, it's something nearer to home. It's a family matter, you know.'

'Then it must be about Dorothea,' Celia said quickly. 'What has happened? What has she done now?'

'It all started with Casaubon's will,' Mr Brooke said unhappily. 'That was a mistake, you know. It made everything worse.'

'For God's sake, tell us what you are talking about!' Sir James cried.

'Dorothea is going to be married again, you know,' Mr Brooke said unhappily.

Sir James' face went white with anger. Celia looked first at her husband and then at her uncle.

'Is it Mr Ladislaw?' she said.

'Yes, she will marry Ladislaw,' Mr Brooke replied.

'When did you hear this?' Sir James asked.

After the Storm

'Yesterday, when I went to Lowick, you know. Dorothea sent for me. It all happened quite suddenly. I can't stop it, you know.'

'I knew this would happen,' Sir James said angrily. 'I told you to send Ladislaw away. The marriage will take Dorothea away from her proper place in society. She will be poor – married to that man – a foreigner with no position in society at all.'

'I told her that,' Mr Brooke said. 'But Dorothea has thought of everything. She hates Mr Casaubon's money and she has some of her own, you know.'

'Dorothea said she would never marry again,' Celia said. 'And now, I suppose, she is going to be married very soon?'

'In three weeks,' Mr Brooke replied. 'We must make the best of it, I suppose.'

When Mr Brooke had left, Celia spoke to her husband,

'I would like to have the carriage to go to Lowick,' she said. 'I must speak to Dorothea at once. Perhaps I can make her change her mind.'

Dorothea was in her own room when her sister arrived.

'Oh, Celia, I am delighted to see you!' she cried. 'I was afraid that you would not come.'

Celia sat down and looked at her sister sadly.

'We are all very disappointed,' Celia said. 'You always want things that are not right. First you marry an old man, clever and rich, but ugly and very boring. Now you want to marry Mr Ladislaw who has no land or money at all. You always want to make yourself uncomfortable, in some way or another, don't you, my dear?

'Sir James is so angry too,' Celia went on. 'You will go away and perhaps I shall never see you again! And my poor little Arthur will never know his aunt.'

'Dear Celia,' Dorothea said, 'if that happens, it will not be my fault.'

'Yes, it will,' Celia replied. 'James won't see you, because all this is so wrong. So I won't be able to see you either. And where are you going to live?'

'I'm going to London,' Dorothea replied. 'That is where Will's work is.'

'But you will have to live in a house on a street!' Celia cried. 'This is another of your mistakes, Dorothea. You said that you were never going to marry again.'

'Well, now I am going to marry Mr Ladislaw,' Dorothea said in a clear voice. 'I have promised to marry him and that's what I am going to do.'

Celia sighed. She knew that when her sister spoke like that, nothing would change her mind.

'Is Mr Ladislaw very fond of you?' Celia asked.

'I hope so. I am very fond of him,' Dorothea replied with a smile.

'Well that's good. I do so wonder how it all happened. Can't you tell me, Dorothea dear?'

Dorothea laughed.

'No, Celia, I can't,' she said. 'You would never believe me if I did!'

22

What Came Afterwards

Nicholas Bulstrode was getting ready to leave Middlemarch, where he felt that he could no longer live. His wife had supported him when the town had turned against him. He decided that he must help her and her family, the Vincys, if he could.

'I am not selling my land, Harriet,' he said. 'I am leaving it to you in my will. Is there anything else that you would like me to do?'

'I would like you to help my brother's family, Nicholas,' Harriet

What Came Afterwards

Bulstrode replied. 'My brother says that my niece, Rosamond, and Doctor Lydgate are leaving Middlemarch too. They are young and have their whole lives in front of them. Give them enough to make those lives easier, wherever they are.'

'Mr Lydgate does not wish me to help him,' Bulstrode replied. 'He has returned the money I sent him and accepted Mrs Casaubon's offer of help. But I have another plan. Your brother's son, Fred, has been doing well lately. He has been working with Caleb Garth and the young man is now a good farm-manager. I would like him to look after the farm at Stone Court. In time, Fred will have the chance to own the farm himself. He can marry and settle down. Speak to your brother about it Harriet.'

'Thank you, I will,' Harriet Bulstrode replied. 'I have always been fond of my brother and he has had a lot of trouble recently. Fred is a good boy. He and Mary Garth have been in love for years. I would like to see them married at last. I would like to see them happy.'

So Fred Vincy got his chance. He worked hard and in a year's time, he and Mary Garth were married.

Fred and Mary Vincy were happy and their marriage was a successful one. They had three children – all boys – and lived at Stone Court for the rest of their long lives.

The future for Tertius and Rosamond was not as happy, although Lydgate became a very successful doctor in London, where many of his patients were from wealthy society families. He died when he was only fifty, leaving Rosamond and his four children with more than enough money to live on.

Rosamond's second husband was a much older doctor who gave his wife her own way in everything. She had a large house, a carriage of her own and money to spend on herself. She and her children were happy.

'Finally I have what I deserve,' Rosamond said to herself. 'All my problems are behind me at last.'

Dorothea had been happy to give up money and position to

What Came Afterwards

marry Will Ladislaw and they worked together for the good of society. In time, Will became a member of Parliament and, with his wife's help, he worked for reform and to improve the lives of people everywhere. English society was changing fast and the Ladislaws were part of that change.

Sir James Chettam continued to oppose the marriage and, at first, he would have nothing to do with the Ladislaws. But Mr Brooke wrote to them every week and, after nearly a year, he sent them an invitation to visit him at Tipton Grange.

Then, one morning, Celia received a letter at Freshitt Hall and when she had read it, she began to cry.

'My dear Celia! What is the matter?' Sir James asked her. 'Have you had bad news?'

Celia shook her head.

'Dorothea has had a little boy and that is good news,' she said, 'But I suppose that you will not let me go and see her! She was very ill and they thought that she would die. Oh, I wish that you were not so unkind, James! I do so want to see Dorothea and the little boy too. But how can I, when you have forbidden me to visit them?'

'I will take you to London tomorrow if that's what you want!' Sir James said quickly.

'I do, yes I do,' Celia replied. 'Dorothea knows nothing about babies and she is short-sighted too. Something will go wrong if I am not there, I know it will.'

Where sisters love each other, their husbands must learn to be friends too. Will Ladislaw and Sir James Chettam had different opinions about most things, but, for the sake of their wives, the two men learnt to be polite to one another.

Mr and Mrs Ladislaw were always invited to the Grange twice a year and, as time went by, their two children looked forward to playing with their little cousins at Freshitt Hall.

Mr Brooke lived to a good age and Dorothea's son inherited his estate.

Dorothea's ideas did not change as she grew older and she

always kept her youthful enthusiasm and her desire to help people. She tried her best to do good in the world and the world was a better place because of it.

Dorothea's life had been an unusual one and some people thought that both her marriages had been mistakes. But her life with Will was very happy and her feelings for him never changed. Dorothea's feelings for the other people she loved did not change either. They only became stronger. Her family and friends loved and respected her until the day she died, and that was enough to complete a happy and successful life.

Points for Understanding

1

1 Dorothea and Celia were different in several ways. List their differences.
2 What have you learned about the sisters' lives so far in this chapter?
3 Dorothea and Celia's uncle had two guests to dinner that evening. What did we learn about the two men?

2

1 Dorothea made an important decision in this chapter. What was it and why did her sister and her uncle not agree with her? What is your opinion?

3

1 Would you have liked to live in Middlemarch? Give reasons for your answer.
2 What did you learn about Mr Casaubon and his family from this chapter?
3 Mr Casaubon and Will Ladislaw did not like each other. Explain why.

4

1 Why had Doctor Lydgate come to Middlemarch?
2 Choose three people mentioned in this chapter and give their opinions of the young doctor.
3 What else did you learn about him?
4 What did you learn about Fred and his sister Rosamond?
5 Would you like Fred and Rosamond as friends? Give reasons for your answers.

5

1. Why was Dorothea so unhappy?
2. Both Dorothea and her husband had been angry earlier that day. Why was this?
3. What did you learn about Will and his cousin, Edward Casaubon, from this chapter?

6

1. Dorothea thought that her marriage might have been a mistake. Why did she think this? Do you agree with her?
2. Celia had some news for her sister. What was it and what do you think about it?
3. Dorothea and her husband had a argument. What was it about?
4. What effect did the argument have on Edward Casaubon?
5. What did Doctor Lydgate tell Dorothea about her husband's illness and why did she blame herself for it?
6. Will was invited to Tipton Grange, but not to Lowick Manor. Why?

7

1. Who was Peter Featherstone and what kind of man was he?
2. How did Fred, Mary Garth and Rosamond think his death would affect them?
3. Lydgate was not planning to become engaged but at the end of this chapter, he was. How did that happen?

8

1. Why did so many people go to Peter Featherstone's funeral, although no one liked him?
2. Why was Dorothea so worried when she heard that Will Ladislaw was staying with her uncle?
3. Why did Featherstone's will surprise everyone except Joshua Rigg?

4 What advice did Mary give to Fred?
5 Why didn't Mr Vincy want Rosamond to marry Lydgate?
6 How did Rosamond persuade her father that she should marry the young doctor?

9

1 What were Mr Brooke's political ideas and why did Sir James disagree with them?
2 Will Ladislaw was helping Mr Brooke. Why did this annoy Mr Casaubon?
3 What did Will talk to Dorothea about when they met?
4 Mr Casaubon wrote to Will. What did he tell him?
5 How did Dorothea make the situation between the cousins worse?

10

1 Why were Mr Brooke's friends worried about him?
2 Mr Casaubon was worried and unhappy for several reasons. What were they?
3 What did he plan to do?
4 What did this plan tell you about Mr Casaubon's character?
5 At the end of the chapter, Dorothea felt sorry for her husband. Why? Do you think that she was right?

11

1 Dorothea felt confused and unhappy and Will was angry. What made them feel like that?
2 What did Rosamond tell her husband about Will? Do you think that she was right?
3 Casaubon asked Dorothea to make him a promise. Why did she not agree at once?
4 Why was Dorothea never able to agree to her husband's request?

12

1 Casaubon added some instructions to his will before he died. What were they and how did Dorothea find out about them?
2 How did these instructions change Dorothea's feelings?
3 Mr Brooke made a speech to the people of Middlemarch. What did they think about it and what did they do?
4 Will and Dorothea had strong feelings for each other. Why didn't they tell each other how they felt?

13

1 What problems did Tertius Lydgate have at that time?
2 What happened when Lydgate tried to tell his wife about those problems?
3 What do you think about the way that Rosamond behaved?

14

1 Why did Rosamond tell the story about Mr Casaubon's will to Will Ladislaw?
2 Will made a decision. What was it?
3 Dorothea and Will met again. What did they learn about each other? Did they tell each other the truth?

15

1 How did the people of Middlemarch feel about Mr Bulstrode?
2 Bulstrode had a secret from his past. What was it and who reminded him of it?
3 The Lydgates were in debt. What different ideas did Lydgate and Rosamond have about solving the problem?

16

1 How had Bulstrode harmed Will Ladislaw in the past?
2 Why did Bulstrode think that he would have to leave Middlemarch?
3 Why did Will Ladislaw reject Bulstrode's offer of money?
4 Lydgate asked Bulstrode to help him. What advice did Bulstrode give to the young doctor?

17

1 Raffles had become ill. What treatment did Lydgate advise Bulstrode to give him?
2 Bulstrode changed his mind about helping Lydgate. Why do you think he did that?
3 Raffles died. How did that happen and who was to blame?

18

1 Rosamond Lydgate and Harriet Bulstrode behaved differently when they heard about their husbands' troubles. Explain how.
2 What did Rosamond feel about Will Ladislaw?

19

1 Dorothea decided to help the Lydgates. Why? What did she do?
2 What did Dorothea think when she saw Rosamond and Will together?
3 Will told Rosamond his true feelings. What were they?

20

1 The next morning, Dorothea and Rosamond had a conversation. Why was that conversation important for both of them?
2 Later, Rosamond wrote Will a note. What did she tell him and what did Will think?

21

1 What happened when Will and Dorothea met in the library?
2 Dorothea said 'Nothing else matters now'. What did she mean?
3 What did Dorothea's family think about her decision? Do you agree?

22

1 Most of the characters were happy at the end of the book. Explain how that happened.

Glossary

1 **estate** (page 4)
a very large area of land that belongs to one person, usually with a very big house on it.
2 **boarding school** (page 4)
a school in which most or all of the students live during the part of the year that they have lessons.
3 **intellectual** (page 4)
a person who is well educated and interested in art, science, literature etc. at an advanced level.
4 **gossip** – *to gossip* (page 5)
to talk or have a conversation about other people or about things that are not important, or about other people's private lives.
5 **criticised** – *to criticise* (page 5)
to say what you think is wrong or bad about something. Comments that show that you think something is wrong or bad are called *criticisms*.
6 **reform bill** (page 5)
a *bill* is a written document containing a proposal for a new law. A *reform* is a change that is made in order to improve a situation or system. The Reform Bill of 1832 was designed to change the Government's voting system.
7 **Parliament** (page 5)
the main law-making institution in some countries. In the UK, Parliament consists of politicians elected to the House of Commons and members of the House of Lords.
8 **inferior** (page 6)
not as good as something else.
9 **rebel** (page 6)
someone who opposes people in authority or opposes accepted ways of doing things.
10 **ambition** (page 6)
something that you very much want to do, usually something that is difficult to achieve.
11 **cottage** (page 8)
an old, small house, usually in a village or the countryside.
12 **jewel** (page 8)
a hard, coloured, and usually valuable stone that has been cut and made shiny. Examples of jewels are *emeralds* and *amethysts*. An *emerald* is a

bright green stone, and an *amethyst* is a purple stone. These stones are used in valuable *jewellery* – objects that you wear as decoration. Types of jewellery include *rings*, which you wear on your finger, *bracelets*, which you wear on your wrist, and *necklaces*, which you wear around your neck.

13 **blushed** – *to blush* (page 8)
if you blush, your cheeks become red because you feel embarrassed or ashamed.

14 **praise** – *to praise* (page 9)
to express strong approval or admiration for someone or something, especially in public.

15 **orphan** (page 9)
a child whose parents have died.

16 **guardian** (page 9)
someone who is legally responsible for another person such as a child whose parents have died.

17 **governess** (page 9)
a woman whose job was to look after and teach her employer's children in their home, especially in the past.

18 **inherited** – *to inherit something* (page 10)
to receive property or money from someone who has died.

19 **Reverend** (page 10)
a title used for some Christian priests and ministers.

20 **scholar** (page 10)
someone who studies a particular subject and knows a lot about it, especially a subject that is not scientific.

21 **myth** (page 11)
an ancient traditional story about gods, heroes, and magic. A collection of ancient myths, especially those of a particular country or religion, is called a *mythology*. Mr Casaubon wants to write a *key* – a list of meanings – which will explain all of the myths of the world and show that they are connected.

22 **bachelor** (page 12)
a man who has never been married. It is more usual to say that someone who is not married is single.

23 **flattered** – *to flatter* (page 12)
feeling pleased that someone notices and admires you.

24 **companion** (page 13)
a friend who you spend a lot of time with.

25 **honoured** (page 13)
used for saying that you are proud to be able to do something.

26 **honour** – *to honour* (page 13)
   to have or show respect for someone.
27 **engaged** (page 15)
   if two people are engaged, they have formally agreed to get married.
28 **manufacturer** (page 16)
   manufacture is the process of making goods in large quantities in a factory. A *manufacturer* is a person or company that manufactures a product.
29 **tradesman** (page 16)
   someone who sells goods or services.
30 **portrait** (page 17)
   a painting, drawing, or photograph of someone, especially of their face only.
31 **preached** – *to preach* (page 18)
   to talk about a religious subject at a religious meeting, especially in church.
32 **bowed** – *to bow* (page 18)
   to bend your body forwards from the waist, especially to show respect for someone.
33 **settle down** – *to settle down* (page 20)
   to begin to live a quieter life by getting married or staying permanently in a place.
34 **honeymoon** (page 20)
   a holiday that two people take after they get married.
35 **manuscript** (page 20)
   a very old book or document written by hand before books began to be printed.
36 **Vatican** – *The Vatican* (page 20)
   the *Vatican City*, in Rome, is the smallest independent nation in the world and the headquarters of the Roman Catholic Church.
37 **surgeon** (page 21)
   a doctor who is trained to perform operations involving cutting, usually in a hospital.
38 **patient** (page 21)
   someone who is receiving medical treatment.
39 **sympathetic** (page 21)
   kind to someone who has a problem and willing to understand how they feel.
40 **baronet** (page 21)
   a man who is a member of the British nobility – people in the highest social class who usually have titles. A *baronet* has a lower status than a baron.

41 *elegant* (page 22)
   an elegant person is attractive and graceful in their appearance and behaviour.
42 *embroider* – *to embroider* (page 22)
   to decorate cloth with a design of coloured stitches. The activity of decorating cloth with coloured stitches is called *embroidery*.
43 *degree* (page 23)
   a course of study at a university, or the qualification that you get after completing the course.
44 *way* – *to get/have your (own) way* (page 24)
   to be allowed to have or do what you want.
45 *charm* (page 24)
   a personal quality that attracts people to you and makes them like you.
46 *cholera* (page 24)
   a serious disease affecting your stomach and intestines (=the long tube that carries waste out of your body) that often causes death. It is caused by drinking water or eating food infected with bacteria.
47 *dedication* (page 26)
   the large amount of time and effort that someone spends on something.
48 *enthusiasm* (page 26)
   the feeling of being very interested in something or excited by it.
49 *material* (page 26)
   information, ideas, and experiences that you use as the subject of a book, film, song etc.
50 *dictate* – *to dictate* (page 26)
   to say the words of a document that someone else will write or type for you.
51 *profession* (page 28)
   a job that you need special skills and qualifications to do, especially one with high social status.
52 *couch* (page 33)
   a long low comfortable seat that two or three people can sit on.
53 *why on earth?* (page 33)
   an expression used for adding emphasis to questions. Sir James is expressing his great surprise that Dorothea agreed to marry Mr Casaubon.
54 *foolish* (page 33)
   lacking good sense and judgment.
55 *case* (page 34)
   an instance of a disease.
56 *anxiety* (page 34)
   a worried feeling you have because you think something bad might happen.

57 **will** (page 35)
   a legal document that explains what you want to happen to your money and possessions after you die.
58 **turning down** – *to turn something/someone down* (page 36)
   to refuse to accept an offer or request.
59 **credit** – *to be a credit to someone* (page 40)
   if you are a credit to someone connected with you, or if you do them credit, they should be proud of you.
60 **lawyer** (page 40)
   someone whose profession is to provide people with legal advice and services.
61 **heir** (page 40)
   someone who will receive money, property, or a title when another person dies.
62 **clergyman** (page 41)
   a man who leads religious services, especially a Christian priest.
63 **warehouse** (page 43)
   a big building where large amounts of goods are stored.
64 **insure** – *to insure something* (page 44)
   if an insurance company *insures* you or something you own, they accept money from you and agree to pay you if you die or are ill or injured. Or if something you own is damaged, lost, or stolen. Mr Vincy asks Lydgate to insure his life, so that Rosamond will have enough money if her husband dies.
65 **radical** (page 44)
   radical opinions are based on the belief that important political or social changes are necessary.
66 **pioneer** (page 44)
   one of the first people to do something important that is later continued and developed by other people. The name of the newspaper shows that it is published by people who want political change.
67 **article** (page 45)
   a piece of writing about a particular subject that is published in a newspaper or magazine.
68 **butler** (page 46)
   the most important male servant in a rich person's house, whose job is to organize the other servants, to welcome guests, to pour wine at meals etc.
69 **disinherited** – *to disinherit* (page 47)
   to make legal arrangements so that a close relative, especially your son or daughter, will not receive any of your money or property when you die.

70 *refugee* (page 47)
someone who has to leave their country, especially during a war or other threatening event.
71 **forbidden** – *to forbid something* (page 53)
to tell someone that they must not do something.
72 *stubborn* (page 53)
a stubborn person is not willing to change their ideas or consider anyone else's reasons or arguments.
73 **honourable** (page 53)
morally good and deserving respect.
74 **symptom** (page 55)
a sign that someone has an illness.
75 **curse** – *to curse* (page 57)
to say or think offensive or impolite words about someone or something.
76 **adores** – *to adore* (page 58)
to love someone very much.
77 *microscope* (page 58)
a piece of equipment for looking at things that are too small to see normally.
78 **bonnet** (page 62)
a hat that ties under your chin.
79 **shawl** (page 62)
a large piece of material that is worn by a woman around her shoulders or on her head.
80 **summer house** (page 62)
a small building in a garden or park where you can sit in warm weather.
81 **executor** (page 63)
someone who arranges for the instructions of a dead person's will to be followed.
82 **insulted** – *to insult* (page 63)
to say or do something offensive.
83 **widow** (page 65)
a woman whose husband has died. She has not married again.
84 *elector* (page 66)
someone who has the right to vote in an election.
85 **longed** – *to long* (page 70)
to want something very much.
86 **income** (page 70)
money that someone gets from working or from investing money.
87 **barrister** (page 71)
a lawyer in England or Wales who is allowed to speak in the higher law courts.

88 **debt** (page 73)
a situation in which you owe money to other people.
89 **flirt** – *to flirt* (page 73)
to behave towards someone in a way that shows your sexual or romantic interest in them.
90 **entertaining** – *to entertain* (page 74)
to receive someone as a guest and give them food and drink or other forms of enjoyment.
91 **inventory** (page 76)
a list giving details of all the things in a place.
92 **cutlery** (page 77)
the knives, forks, and spoons that you use for eating food.
93 **shutter** (page 82)
a cover that can be closed over the outside of a window.
94 **pawnbroker** (page 86)
someone whose job is to lend money to people in exchange for a valuable object that they can sell if the person does not return the money.
95 **agent** (page 87)
a person or company that does business for another person or company, for example by selling their products or by dealing with their customers.
96 **sins** (page 92)
an action, thought, or way of behaving that is wrong according to religious laws.
97 **practice** (page 94)
the business of a doctor, lawyer, or other professional person.
98 **bankrupt** (page 95)
someone who has officially admitted that they have no money and cannot pay what they owe.
99 **bailiff** (page 97)
an official whose job is to take away the possessions of someone who has not paid money they owe.
100 **opium** (page 98)
a powerful illegal drug made from the seeds of a type of poppy (=flower). Opium was used in the past as a medicine for reducing pain.
101 **bribe** (page 101)
money or a present given to someone so that they will help you by doing something dishonest or illegal.
102 **resign** – *to resign* (page 102)
to state formally that you are leaving a job permanently.

Dictionary extracts adapted from the Macmillan English Dictionary © Bloomsbury Publishing PLC 2002 and © A & C Black Publishers Ltd 2005.

Further Study Questions

Plot

1 Make a list of the main actions and events in the novel. Think about:
   a) marriage proposals
   b) deaths
   c) money changing hands
   d) conversations and arguments

   Choose the five most important events from your list. Describe the results of each event and explain why each one is important to the story.

2 Letters play an important part in the plot. Think of five letters. Explain who wrote them, why they wrote them and what the reaction was to the letter. Think about how each letter affects the plot.

3 Wills also play an important part in the plot. What did Peter Featherstone's will say? Who did it affect and how? Think about Edward Casaubon's will. How did this affect the relationship between Dorothea and Will Ladislaw? What does it tell us about the power of money and property in society at that time?

4 Why are Bulstrode and Ladislaw's pasts kept secret? Who might they offend or affect? Why? Discuss the role of gossip and secrets in the novel. What do they show about the society of Middlemarch?

Essay question

Prepare to write an answer to this question.

> Think about the events and actions of the novel. Explain how they relate to Eliot's full original title of *Middlemarch: a study of provincial life*.

Before you start writing, choose three or four important events and make notes about what they tell us about life in Middlemarch (see pp 4–7 for information about English society at the time the novel was written).

Characters

1 Choose adjectives from the box below to describe the characters. Give examples from the novel to explain your choices.

> honest   selfish   foolish   jealous   boring   serious
> stubborn   sensible   romantic

   a) Dorothea Brooke
   b) Edward Casaubon
   c) Nicholas Bulstrode
   d) Rosamund Vincy
   e) Tertius Lydgate
   f) Will Ladislaw

2 Which characters do you sympathise with most? Why? Are there any characters you don't sympathise with?

3 Explain the relationship between the characters below and the six main characters in (1).

   a) Celia Brooke
   b) Mr Brooke
   c) Sir James Chettam
   d) Fred Vincy
   e) Mary Garth
   f) John Raffles

   What do these characters tell us about the main characters and about life in Middlemarch?

   Example: *a) Celia is Dorothea's sister. She is very different from her sister both in her personality and in her choice of husband. She is a typical woman of her age. She makes a good marriage and is happy in her role as wife and mother. The people of Middlemarch understand and approve of her conventional decisions. Dorothea's decisions on the other hand are more difficult to understand. She doesn't enjoy elegant dresses or jewels, she marries a man twice her age who uses her as a servant and then she gives up most of her money to marry for love. She isn't happy to be a wife and mother and accept her position in society. She tries to use her money and position to do good for others.*

4 Compare the following pairs of characters. Think about their position in society, the decisions they make and the results of those decisions.

   a) Dorothea Brooke and Rosamund Vincy
   b) Will Ladislaw and Edward Casaubon
   c) Tertius Lydgate and Nicholas Bulstrode

Essay question

Prepare to write an answer to this question.

> 'There are no heroes or villains in Middlemarch, only ordinary people, living ordinary lives'.

Write a short essay in response to the statement above. Describe three main characters. Discuss to what extent they represent 'ordinary people' and who they represent in Eliot's 'Study of provincial life'.

Before you start writing make notes in the table below.

Name	In what way are they ordinary?	Who do they represent?
1 *Dorothea*	*dependent on husband*	*daughters of rich landowners expected to make a good marriage*
2		
3		

Themes

1 **Marriage**

   a) Discuss these quotations about marriage and money.

   'Every girl owes it to her family and to herself to make a good marriage. To marry a poor man is always a great mistake.'

   Why is it a 'mistake' to marry a poor man? How can it affect the family?

   'Marriage is a very expensive business.'

   Is it expensive only in financial terms, or is there also a more personal price to pay?

   b) Think about the marriages of Dorothea and Casaubon and Rosamund and Lydgate. Why could they be considered 'unfortunate marriages'? What did each character expect to get out of their marriages? Why did their marriages fail?

2. **Women's position in society**
   a) Think about the role of women in Middlemarch society and how this role is described in the novel. In what way are the following women a positive example to other women?
   Mary Garth, Harriet Bulstrode.
   b) In what way are the following women victims of their position in society?
   Dorothea Brooke, Rosamund Vincy.

3. **The power of money and property**
   a) Think about how the following people put their money to bad use: Peter Featherstone, Edward Casaubon, Nicholas Bulstrode, Mr Brooke.
   b) Think about the problems that money creates for the following characters: Fred Vincy, Tertius Lydgate, Dorothea Brooke, Rosamund Vincy. How do they deal with these problems?
   c) Think about how Dorothea Brooke, Edward Casaubon, Mr Brooke and Nicholas Bulstrode try to help people with their money. What are the results of their actions?

4. **Ideals vs reality**
   a) What are the following characters' main ambitions?
      a) Dorothea Brooke   b) Edward Casaubon
      c) Rosamund Vincy   d) Tertius Lydgate

      Compare what they wanted to do and what they actually succeeded in doing. To what extent did they fail in their ambitions? Why? What problems did they have to deal with?
   b) Think about other characters and their ambitions. Think about Nicholas Bulstrode's attempts to build a new life for himself, Mr Brooke's plans to become a member of parliament and Fred Vincy's studies and career.

Essay questions

Choose one of the following questions and write a full answer.

Q1 Think about the significance of money in Middlemarch. Comment on the good and bad uses of money in the novel and discuss how it affects people's choices.

Q2 Discuss the difficulties involved in 'making a good marriage'. Think about the difference between what people are looking for in a marriage and the reality of married life. Take two examples from the novel and describe the problems experienced by the two couples.

Q3 Give a brief description of the class structure in Middlemarch. Think about the various families described, the contact between them and how their lives are connected.

For help with answering these questions, visit www.macmillanenglish.com/readers

For more information and free resources visit:
www.macmillanenglish.com/readers

MACMILLAN READERS

Macmillan Education
The Macmillan Building
4 Crinan Street
London N1 9XW
A division of Macmillan Publishers Limited
Companies and representatives throughout the world

ISBN 978-0-230-02686-5

This version of *Middlemarch* was retold by Margaret Tarner.
First published 2008
Text © Macmillan Publishers Limited 2008
Design and illustration © Macmillan Publishers Limited 2008
This version first published 2008

All rights reserved; no part of this publication may be
reproduced, stored in a retrieval system, transmitted in any
form, or by any means, electronic, mechanical, photocopying,
recording, or otherwise, without the prior written permission of
the publishers.

Illustrated by Roberto Tomei
Cover by Rex Features

Printed and bound in Thailand

2018 2017 2016
9 8 7 6 5 4